The Daughter as Reader

The Daughter as Reader

ENCOUNTERS BETWEEN LITERATURE AND LIFE

Paula Marantz Cohen

Ann Arbor

THE UNIVERSITY OF MICHIGAN PRESS

Copyright © by the University of Michigan 1996
All rights reserved
Published in the United States of America by
The University of Michigan Press
Manufactured in the United States of America
⊗ Printed on acid-free paper
1999   1998   1997   1996   4   3   2   1

A CIP catalogue record for this book is available from the British Library.

"Poetry and Sexual Harassment" first appeared in the *Cimarron Review*
98 (January 1992) and is reprinted here with the permission of the Board
of Regents for Oklahoma State University, holders of the copyright.
"Confessions of a Literary Daughter" appeared in an earlier form in the
Iowa Review 22, no. 1 (1992), under the title "Reply to my Father: Confessions of a Feminist Critic." It is reprinted here by permission.

Library of Congress Cataloging-in-Publication Data

Marantz Cohen, Paula, 1953–
    The daughter as reader : encounters between literature and life /
Paula Marantz Cohen.
        p.   cm.
    Includes bibliographical references.
    ISBN 0-472-10693-7 (hardcover : acid-free paper)
    1. Marantz Cohen, Paula, 1953–   . 2. Critics—United States—
Biography. 3. Feminists—United States—Biography. 4. Authors—
Books and reading. I. Title.
PN75.M24A3   1996
809—dc20
    [B]   95-40044
                                                          CIP

For my parents

Acknowledgments

I want to express my gratitude to the colleagues, friends, and family members who helped me complete this book. Elaine DeLancey, Julia Epstein, Beth Kowaleski-Wallace, Gertrude Penziner, Burton Porter, and Thomas Travisano generously read and critiqued earlier drafts of individual essays. Rosetta Marantz Cohen, Mark Greenberg, Dave Jones, and Samuel Scheer read the entire manuscript and offered advice on revision. My husband, Alan S. Penziner, has been my intellectual touchstone and emotional support, and my children, Sam and Kate Marantz Penziner, have been a source of inspiration and joy. My greatest debt is to my parents, Ruth and Murray Marantz Cohen, whose voices, engaged in a never-ending, always interesting argument, are behind these essays.

Contents

Introduction   1

Poetry and Sexual Harassment   5

"To Hell with Dying"   15

Sisters   23

Turning the Screw on Dr. Spock   35

Anorexic Thinking   45

The Good Class   57

Speech and Silence   65

Rx for Premature Labor: Reading Trollope   77

The Marriage Plot   89

Born to Shop   97

On Reading Proust   107

"Makin' Whoopee": The Art of Female Self-Performance   117

Love and Pity   125

The Birth and Death of the Unconscious   135

Confessions of a Literary Daughter   143

On the Other Hand   151

Notes   155

Introduction

$\mathcal{T}$ HE title of this collection, *The Daughter as Reader*, carries a number of different but interconnected meanings. The first has to do with the way in which reading is associated for me with my role as a daughter in my parents' house. My parents saw reading as a sacred rite. As long as I was engrossed in a good book, I was permitted to stretch out on the living room couch and read the afternoon away—all chores and responsibilities were suspended, all calls from the outer world muted or blocked. I have never been able to recreate such a protected space in which to read. Especially now that I have children of my own, I can no longer stretch out undisturbed on the couch; I am forced to read in offices and libraries, made subject to time constraints, and confined to straight-backed chairs. Still, reading remains a privileged activity in my life. It is my way of combining a sense of achievement with a sense of pleasure and security, and I see my work as a professional reader (that is, a teacher and critic) as an extension of a childhood idyll.

Another meaning of "the daughter as reader" concerns the way in which I think of myself as a daughter *of* literature. As a child, I lived under the impression that my real life had not yet begun. I read novels with a vague sense that they were preparations for life. What was I looking for? The novels I read were not about adventure and exploration; they were mostly about the rituals of domestic life and courtship. Yet what they taught me is perhaps best encapsulated in the advice on marriage given by the hero to the heroine in Jane Austen's *Northanger Abbey:* marriage is like dancing, he explains; the object in both is for the partners "to keep their own imaginations from wandering towards the perfections of their neighbours, or fancying that they should have been better off with anyone else." The object, in other words, is to interpret generously and within limits, using what one has at hand. When I read William Wordsworth in college and found him arguing for an appreciation of ordinary life (of the yew tree, and the leech-gatherer, and Lucy who lived unknown), I realized that he was doing with nature and simple human relationships what Jane Austen did with manners and marriage and what Henry James did with the nuances of language. Each of these authors taught me how to find interest and inspiration in seemingly small and insignificant facets of experience.

Finally, my title refers to my position as a daughter to a particular group of books. The literature in which I was schooled in college and in a good part of graduate school was built on a system of values in which men had authority and women—and particularly daughters—were without authority. Even the novels by women that I read as a girl appeared to support this unequal division of power. These books conditioned me in a daughterly role that I have since come to resent and that I still feel limits me. But, insofar as they also taught me to read critically, to doubt, and to subvert established opinion, I owe to them much of my ability to resent them, to read them in new ways, and to supplement or replace them with other books and ways of thinking.

The notion that certain books can serve to direct and shape experience has been propounded by literary critics for a long time. Matthew Arnold called literature a "criticism of life" and argued that reading could lead to cultural and social improvement. Wordsworth, he maintained, would have been a better poet had he read more books, and England would be a better place if it were a nation of readers. Lionel Trilling, Arnold's twentieth-century disciple, extended this thinking into a more modern context. He drew on nineteenth-century literature to help him sort through the confusion of politics, economics, and ego in which he saw his own culture engulfed.

But for all that critics like Arnold and Trilling sought to use literature to give form and meaning to social experience, it took female critics to personalize that critique, to acknowledge that the self, too, could be formed or, as the case may be, *de*formed, by a literary tradition. Virginia Woolf's pioneering entry into the genre, *A Room of One's Own*, was not just a critique of the sexist assumptions of her culture as it expressed itself in its national literature; it was also a new style of criticism in which its author made herself present on the page: an erudite, ironic, sometimes bitter, meanderingly casual self. When Woolf, writing in the first person, describes being barred from Oxbridge Library by an officious beadle, it is not just shame and anger for her sex but shame and anger for herself that get registered. Many contemporary feminist critics who launched their careers trying to be as rigorously abstract as their male counterparts have begun to do what Woolf did in 1929: to loosen what Jane Tompkins has called the "straitjacket of theory" and speak as themselves. Woolf taught that this is not really about discarding one thing for something else but about mixing voices and shifting emphases—making the sentence and the subject matter fit the writer rather than cramp and deform her.

The essays in this volume are a contribution to that hybrid genre that I trace back to Virginia Woolf. As such, they don't resemble other works of autobiographical literary criticism and will probably be faulted for not doing enough of one thing or for doing too much of something else. The mix of autobiography and literary criticism is, by definition, an uneasy and risky one, and hence the likelihood exists that I will offend or dissatisfy some readers. When I think of some of the more memorable practitioners in this genre—Woolf, Adrienne Rich, Rachel M. Brownstein, Gloria Anzaldúa, Alice Walker, Camille Paglia—I acknowledge that each can irritate me in a different way and to a different degree, depending upon the topic addressed and my mood at the moment of reading. What they share, however, is a determination to risk being themselves on the page—or, perhaps more accurately, to risk asserting something as dubious and elusive as a self on the page. This is as exciting and interesting as it can sometimes be irritating.

I intend these essays for people who are not necessarily academics or even feminists. They are for lovers of books who are also seeking to make meaning out of the clutter of daily life. My hope is that the essays may spark a line of thought, evoke a personal experience, elicit an argument, or recall a book once read with pleasure—in short, I hope they will encourage readers to extend into their own lives the personal acts of literary appropriation that I record.

Poetry and Sexual Harassment

They Flee from Me

They flee from me, that sometime did me seek,
With naked foot stalking in my chamber.
I have seen them, gentle, tame, and meek,
That now are wild, and do not remember
That sometime they put themselves in danger
To take bread at my hand, and now they range,
Busily seeking with a continual change.

Thanked be Fortune it hath been otherwise,
Twenty times better; but once in special,
In thin array, after a pleasant guise,
When her loose gown from her shoulders did fall,
And she me caught in her arms long and small,
And therewith all sweetly did me kiss
And softly said, "Dear heart, how like you this?"

It was no dream, I lay broad waking.
But all is turned, thorough my gentleness,
Into a strange fashion of forsaking;
And I have leave to go, of her goodness,
And she also to use newfangleness.
But since that I so kindely am served.
I fain would know what she hath deserved.

*C*HIS poem by Sir Thomas Wyatt, written during the early six-
teenth century, has always been among my favorite poems. I
remember reading it for the first time in college and then reading it
over and over again to anyone who would listen. This was during that
period of my life when I believed that the books and records I liked dis-
tilled some essence of me and had to be pressed on others as part of

introducing myself to them. The Wyatt poem was melodious, but it was also relatively obscure in its meaning; it lent itself to being read aloud and then discussed heatedly late at night in the dorm. But what I liked especially about the poem was the way in which the poet (the poem seemed to demand that I equate the persona of the speaker with the poet) exposed himself to his readers, made visible the ingredients of his mood: the sense of loss, the hurt pride, the nostalgia for the particular moments of past experience, the bitterness—these were all palpably present and very moving to an undergraduate. The poem seemed to me a superb example of the intense self-awareness that I had learned to associate with Renaissance humanism.

The poem is still a delight to me, but I must say that I read it differently now, many years after first coming across it in college. In between lies my exposure to the feminist movement and, more specifically, my experience with men and authority in the form of boyfriends, teachers, employers, corporate offices, and university faculties. The persona of the poem is far less sympathetic to me: I can hear the strident self-pity of the male ego, where before I only heard the lyrical suffering of an individual. Yet I cannot entirely discard that earlier sympathy either. The poem evokes in me multiple, contradictory feelings of the kind I have toward people I love but whose motives I often suspect. I can explain my present response to the poem best by recounting an experience that engendered a similar response. Only quite a bit later did I come to analyze how I felt about the experience I want to relate, and it is not clear whether coming back to the Wyatt poem helped me to do this or whether the experience, as I gradually came to understand it, conditioned how I later read the poem. I tend to think that the real-life experience and the experience of the poem cannot be separated; each interprets the other.

The incident occurred during my senior year in college, a period of transition between the classicism of my early college years, when I read people and poems quite literally and tended to give them the benefit of the doubt, and my more baroque New York City years, when I assumed a pose of cynicism and world-weariness. I was led to assume this pose largely because I was awakened to the exploitativeness of "patriarchal authority" by the kind of abuse that my friends and I suffered at the hands of men. New York was notorious for throwing up examples of the worst of the species and was full of magazine articles that taught women how to interpret even neutral male behavior as arrogant and abusive.

The incident that I want to recount occurred, then, in the space between innocence and experience. It was the last week of classes during my senior year, and I had handed in my French paper for a course on Surrealism. The paper was on a novel entitled *Nadja* by André Breton, the leader of the Surrealist Movement (Breton and his friends took themselves seriously enough to produce a "manifesto" for their movement, which we had dutifully pored over in the first weeks of the course). Nadja is the name of a young woman who fascinates and eludes the narrator. She seems like a schizophrenic, and, in fact, when she disappears at the end of the novel, it is to enter a mental institution. But clinical traits in the character are vague and largely irrelevant. Nadja is really a conceit by which the author can depict the irrationality, spontaneity, and discontinuity favored by the Surrealist Movement. By using Nadja to embody these qualities, the male persona can present them as powerful and compelling while remaining himself in the privileged narrative position. Thus, though he is unable to possess Nadja imaginatively in his guise as her lover inside the novel, he controls her presentation as her chronicler, making her elusiveness fit his agenda. The book is admired by scholars as a fine example of Surrealist writing, and yet the use of the male voice to record the female Surrealist "body" seems to expose the stereotypical assumptions about gender and power underlying the movement. My classmates and I were not inclined to make such an observation at the time—this was the mid-1970s—and our professor, as I shall explain, was certainly not oriented in this direction.

Now the professor in this course was a man over seventy, a venerable professor of French with an endowed chair. The field in which he had made his mark as a scholar had, it so happens, been the Renaissance, but he had grown restive later in life, and his distinguished reputation had afforded him the freedom to range in his teaching outside his area of expertise. I had taken his Surrealism course because I had heard that he was about to retire. It seemed an exciting prospect to be in his last class and watch him close the book on his career. But, as is often the case with those who have gained eminence within the desultory setting of a university, his reputation had been made at a much earlier date, and his last years as a teacher were not his best. He was no longer especially interested in his subject matter; he wandered; he name-dropped (mostly people we had never heard of); he muddled his words. He was tired. Perhaps he drank (I had heard somewhere that he had lost his wife some years before). But he was a nice man. He had a kind of distracted fondness for literature in general, and he wanted students to do well.

I had gone to his office near the end of the term to collect my paper. It was not, I knew, a particularly good paper. It was written in French, and I was an awkward stylist. Moreover, the Surrealists had not "taken" on me. Try as I would to find an appropriate theory to explain what they were up to, I was not convinced. And if I waived the theory and tried to go with the emotional appeal of their work, I had no success either. It left me cold. It seemed dated and prankish. Perhaps I sensed, though I had not the words for it then, that this was a boys' circle; women were allowed as secondary artists, but they served better as muses, like Nadja, or, more crudely, as bare behinds upon which the shape of a violin could be painted.

All the same, I'd gone to pick up my paper. Although I knew the paper wasn't good, I also thought it wasn't bad. Given the benignity of the instructor and a general weariness that I sensed he had about exerting himself in the grade department, I expected he might give me an A for it. When I entered his office, which was all paneled wood and massive, built-in shelves lined with old, beautifully bound volumes (some of which were already beginning to be piled into large cardboard boxes), he was standing by the window staring out. His expression was wistful. He looked very old. I announced my presence, and he jumped slightly, cleared his throat, and began a rather amorphous flow of talk, part in French, part English. I told him I enjoyed the course, and he became animated, talking garrulously about a course he had taught thirty years before in which the students had met regularly under the tree in the front courtyard and had taken turns reading Ronsard aloud. I asked him for my paper, and he fumbled among a pile of debris on his desk, and, finally—I had to help him sort— plucked out mine. He had given me an A, and, when I asked him what he thought, he said it was a very good paper and that he had submitted it, along with one other from our class, for the French essay prize. I was enormously flattered—

it was so totally unexpected—and I thanked him effusively. It was then that he took my hand and pulled me clumsily toward him, planting a wet, unfocused kiss in the vicinity of my mouth. I pulled away. I was very surprised, a bit shaken, eager to leave, but also eager not to hurt his feelings. I excused myself, said how much I appreciated his giving of his time, thanked him for the paper, and hurried out.

That was it. I didn't see him again. I got an A in the course. I didn't win the essay prize. I read that he died a few years later. But I have often turned over the strange composite of feelings that the encounter in that office left with me. Recently, it occurred to me that the experience relates to my reading of the Wyatt poem. I suppose that nowadays there are people who might have dragged that old professor into a sexual harassment suit, and the thought makes me wince. And yet the man forced himself on me with that slobbery kiss, and, as I saw it then, not on me in particular but on me as a generic, momentarily accessible young woman. Wyatt refers to the spurning of a particular woman in the second and third verses of his poem, but the poem begins significantly by referring to some group of women or women in general who spurn him: "They flee from me who sometime did me seek." A particular woman's behavior pains him most because it reflects his failure to impose his seductive will more generally: it denotes his decline.

The suspicion that I did not, at that moment, exist as an individual in my professor's eyes is part of what is painful in the memory, and it is that feeling that plays a part in what constitutes sexual harassment. To be harassed is to be treated as an object of gratification and not as a subject with desires and antipathies of one's own. Nonetheless, the pathos of the incident and the poem resides precisely in the way a particular woman (me, Wyatt's "she") ceases to be particular and serves as a metaphor for other things. For my professor was perhaps kissing his youth, his dead wife, his lost class that met under that tree in the courtyard. Likewise, Wyatt was lamenting the loss of his ability to inspire love and to take love and, by extension, life, for granted; in the memory of the loose gown and the small arms catching him, he recalls a younger, more indifferent self, and, in recording the loss of that compound of the particular act and the general attitude, he expresses the full implications of his mortality. The bitterness of the poet's voice in the poem directs itself at the particular woman who has spurned him and at women generally, whose responsiveness he once felt assured of, but it is really the change in himself, and change more generally, that he has to blame.

When I arrive at this point in my thinking about the incident and the poem, however, I always turn back. It angers me to recognize how adeptly the poet does shift the blame and how easily I can shift the blame for my professor. The fact is that the poet strikes out angrily at the fact of mortality by painting women as vain, fickle creatures. And, when I think back on the incident with my professor in this mood, I am outraged at his presumption of being able to use me to gratify a momentary desire—whether to recapture lost youth or lost love. I wonder whether he didn't try to gratify other momentary desires throughout his distinguished career in that wood-paneled office. Isn't it as much the loss of the power to gratify one's desires as it is the loss of sexual attractiveness that the poem records? Indeed, not just the loss of power but also the humiliation of a power reversal is at issue:

> But all is turned, thorough my gentleness,
> Into a strange fashion of forsaking;
> And I have leave to go, of her goodness,
> And she also to use newfangleness.

The poet seems to be decrying some form of women's liberation for which, as a result of his alleged "gentleness," he holds himself responsible. The implication: he should have been less soft, exerted his authority more forcefully. Behind Wyatt's poem is an assumption about masculine rights that is part of his feeling of offense. Certainly, men like my professor have historically possessed the endowed chairs, the wood-paneled offices, and, most damaging to the conditioning of posterity, the books. As Anne Elliot, Jane Austen's most wistful heroine, put it, "the pen has been in their hands." What feminist scholars have discerned that makes their relationship to literature so politically fraught, so *un*literary in many ways, is that, in order to comprehend the tradition of Western literature, one must agree to occupy the masculine position while reading. This means that, if one is a woman, one is constrained to read against oneself, to be in complicity with the masculine writer who invariably sets himself against, or at least apart from, the woman who is objectified in his writing. When Wyatt records the turn-ing of the tables, his experience of women getting the upper hand, he still does so within a literary tradition that conditions us to commiser-ate with him—to give him the upper hand through our access to his feelings as the poem's author. To refuse him that pity is to refuse to remain within the space mapped out by the poem, to act as a political terrorist with respect to the poem—to blow it up. What can I do being both a sympathetic reader and a historically conscious woman? The poem asks me to pity the poet and sympathize with his bitterness. But I know that any loss of power is bound to engender bitterness and self-pity in the one who loses it. How can I pity such loss in a man when I know that it is bound up with giving more to women, who have been deprived of too much for too long?

Yet I cannot rest here either. For I recognize that the feeling of loss of power is entwined with all feelings of loss or incipient loss—loss of love, disappointment in work, consciousness of mortality. The pathos of literature and of the human condition to which it speaks is founded on the feeling of loss. This feeling entails being out of sync with one's surroundings and must always involve some kind of distortion or exploitation of what one finds at hand. Something like this recognition is behind John Ruskin's discussion of what he termed the "pathetic fal-lacy" in literature. Ruskin cites a line from a popular novel of his day: "They rowed her in across the rolling foam—The cruel, crawling foam" and then proceeds to explain his problem with it:

> The foam is not cruel, neither does it crawl. The state of mind which attributes to it these characters of living creatures is one in which the reason is unhinged by grief. All violent feelings have the same effect. They produce in us a falseness in all our impressions of external things, which I would generally characterize as the "pathetic fallacy."

But though Ruskin decried the pathetic fallacy and sought strenuously to avoid it in his own writing, even a cursory study of his work shows that he was not successful. There is no avoiding the pathetic fallacy; we infuse what and whom we see with the feelings that happen to be upon us at the moment. We impose ourselves on our surroundings. How, then, do we draw the line between where feelings get expressed and violation happens?

To many it would seem clear that my professor crossed that line. I think so myself. And yet a part of me is not sure. I recall the tight skirts I liked to wear at that time, my tendency to smile and nod at whatever my teachers said, and, in this case, my effusiveness when I heard that my paper had been submitted for a prize. My desire to please, my nervousness, and my seductive getup might have seemed to my professor to be a direct invitation. Who knows but that I might even have had in mind some kind of benign flirtation—perhaps even a subliminal desire to tease with my eagerness and pliancy a man whom I assumed to be incapable (due to his age and the authority of his position) of a direct response.

I can even move beyond this kind of self-interrogation to another level of disinterestedness and erase myself from the scene entirely. Conditioned by a tradition that includes Thomas Wyatt, I can read that kiss as a work of conceptual art, a Surrealist "automatic moment," a poem that has overstepped the bounds of its medium. I can approach it as a disembodied text and cull it for its unexpected insight into the man (as I have done, in fact, for a good portion of this essay). In this mood I feel sorry for my old professor and maybe even wish, in a purely abstract sort of way, that I had kissed back.

But this mood always passes, and I remember the reality of that impressive wood-paneled office and the piles of important books. I recall that my professor did not teach the course well; that his meandering speech was a monologue; that he hadn't listened, as a good teacher should, for the sounds and silences of disagreement, discomfort, and discontent. And I feel sorry for myself as I was then. For, whatever my pretensions, I was a girl in that office who trusted my professor to read me, as I had tried to read the literature he assigned, with some degree of sympathy and care. When critics act amazed at the notion that the poised and self-confident Anita Hill could have let herself in for the kind of abuse she claims, they miss the distance that separates then from now, and they miss the point of her testimony. She was not demanding that she be personally compensated for past abuse; rather, she was testifying to the pedagogical limitations of a man who had been nominated to serve as one of the nation's principal teachers.

In the same way I see my professor's act as a pedagogical betrayal. Teachers presumably occupy their positions because they have been trained to read well. I hold this against my professor, even as I pity him, that he did not grant me the kind of careful, sensitive, and singular reading he would have granted a poem by Ronsard or Wyatt.

"To Hell with Dying"

*M*Y grandfather was the great love of my childhood. He was already long retired when I knew him, and his life held to an uneventful routine that appealed to my child's need for predictability and order. He ate, for example, always at the same time, and his meals were constructed by my grandmother out of a small selection of foods that met his simple but exacting tastes—tastes that resembled my own. Mornings and afternoons were punctuated by walks, the exercise of choice of Eastern European men who had had to adapt to the New York streets, and he took these briskly but never hurriedly, at just the pace that I could happily match. The most important activity of his day was his reading of the *New York Times*. When I would arrive he would generally be at the kitchen table, the *Times* neatly folded so as to expose the editorial page, a glass of hot water and a piece of carefully buttered rye bread in front of him. I would rush into the room and fall on his neck, taking bites from his rye bread, kissing and hugging him wildly. He would laugh and put the paper aside. Though he was rather frail, he seemed to delight in the roughness with which I expressed my affection and was never irritated by my majestic assumption that I always came first.

Everything about him appealed to me. I loved the way he looked. In our family it was said that he resembled Charles Boyer, but it was not the shadow of some former handsomeness that I cherished but the marks of age and familiarity: the mole on his arm, the folds of skin near his neck, the thinning white hair combed back like ribbons, his bony elbows, the ridges of his nails. I delighted in his smallest habits: the way he placed the newspaper beneath his shoes so as not to soil the couch when he took his afternoon nap and the way he handled the salt shaker, carefully tapping with one finger so that the salt fell evenly on his baked potato. I liked how he wrote with the blue fountain pen in a script that still carried an evocation of the Cyrillic alphabet, how he extracted his glasses from their brown leather case, and how he thumbed through the perforated pages of his bankbook.

The only jarring moments I recall experiencing with him occurred during the hypoglycemic episodes (the result of his diabetes) that he occasionally suffered. At such times he would start babbling incoherently, his personality taking on an uncharacteristic aggressiveness and petulance, and my grandmother would run to him with a glass of orange juice and force him to lie down. Once he was calm my role would reassert itself. For it was always me who was expected to run over and kiss and hug him, to make him laugh and assure me that he was back to normal, that it was "nothing." No one, it was said in the family, could bring my grandfather around the way I could.

When I first read Alice Walker's short story "To Hell with Dying," the last in her early collection of stories *In Love and Trouble,* I was reduced to tears without knowing why. It is a fine story, briefly and simply told, but my reaction seemed extreme, until I realized that Walker's story was about my relationship with my grandfather.

The story is recounted by a nameless narrator with obvious affinities to Walker herself—a black woman from a relatively poor but close rural Southern family who (we learn at the end) is completing her doctorate at a university in Massachusetts. This narrator is intent on describing a childhood idyll: her "first love" for an old man named Mr. Sweet, "a diabetic and an alcoholic and a guitar player who lived down the road from us on a neglected cotton farm."

Aside from the fact that both my grandfather and Mr. Sweet were diabetic, it would be hard to come up with two people less alike in background and personal habits. Yet the relationship between the child and the old man that Walker describes evokes my relationship with my grandfather in a number of striking ways. For one thing there is the physical detail through which the child grounds her love: "Mr. Sweet was a tall, thinnish man with thick kinky hair going dead white. He was dark brown, his eyes were very squinty and sort of bluish, and he chewed Brown Mule tobacco." And there is the special concentration on physical attributes that would not ordinarily be considered beautiful but in which the child takes a sensuous delight: "We loved his wrinkles and would draw some on our brows to be like him, and his white hair was my special treasure and he knew it and would never come to visit us just after he had had his hair cut off at the the barber shop." Like me, the child in the story also expresses her affection with a passionate roughness, "burying [her] small fingers into his wooly hair" and hugging, kissing, pinching, and tickling, with no apparent opposition from her subject.

The resemblance between my relationship and that of Walker's narrator goes beyond these things, however, since the story hinges on a more dramatic motif: the child's ritualistic role in averting Mr. Sweet's death. The narrator recalls that at various junctures throughout her growing up the old man was on his deathbed, presumably past all help. Her family would then be sent for. They would rush to the bedside, her father would sweep mourners aside with the bellowing cry, "To hell with dying!" and she and her brother would jump on Mr. Sweet and, through kisses and lavish caresess, revive him. The narrator inserts herself at the center of the ritual: "I was very good at bringing him around, for as soon as I saw that he was struggling to open his eyes I knew he was going to be all right, and so could finish my revival sure of success. As soon as his eyes were open he would begin to smile and that way I knew that I had surely won. . . . When he began to smile I could tickle him in earnest because I was sure that nothing would get in the way of his laughter."

The revival of Mr. Sweet is in one sense a dramatization of the cliché that a child can act as a tonic to an older person—the reason why so many preschool classes are shepherded to nursing homes during the holidays. But the scene also relays the child's conviction that she can allay death if she tries hard enough. Once, when my son had been preoccupied with the idea of dying, he finally resolved his anxiety with a solution: he decided to jump up and down very quickly if he felt death approaching; this would keep his heart going, he was convinced, indefinitely. This kind of magical thinking, unclouded by doubt and common sense, is embedded in the ritual revival of Mr. Sweet that Walker describes: "we had not learned that death was final when it did come. We thought nothing of triumphing over it so many times, and in fact became a trifle contemptuous of people who let themselves be carried away." But this attitude also has philosophical implications. Mr. Sweet's white wiry hair, his wrinkled brown skin, his mustache the color of Spanish moss, his guitar playing, his chronic drunkenness are all dear to the child because she has not yet learned to overlay these things with political, moral, and aesthetic judgments. She has not yet experienced the exploitativeness and thwarting power of the larger society and the inexorability with which time passes. Her magic is thus an expression of her ignorance of society and history.

This sets up an implicit equation within the story that has the force of biblical parable. Freedom and ignorance are the reward and price of innocence; knowledge and limitation are the reward and price of experience. At one point the narrator veers off to give us a few lines on the history of Mr. Sweet's life: he had been, she writes, "ambitious as a boy, wanted to be a doctor or lawyer or sailor, only to find that black men fare better if they are not. The South was a place where a black man could be killed for trying to improve his lot; the laws of segregation kept most black people from ever having decent schools, housing, or jobs." These sentences are the voice of experience; one can see the narrator—Walker as she exists in her essays—on a soapbox, declaiming to a group of activists. But in the context of this kind of social realization much of what so enchanted the child suddenly takes on a different appearance: it becomes an emblem of disappointment and failure. As the narrator succinctly explains it: "he turned to fishing as his only earnest career and guitar-playing as the only claim to doing anything extraordinarily well." What is sweet from the child's vantage point is bitter from the adult's.

My grandfather came to this country alone at the age of nineteen, having lost his family in the pogroms. He had been well-off in Russia, but he had nothing here. He was too refined to engage in the drive and competitiveness of some of his peers, too proud to borrow. He was obliged to work as a presser in the Garment District, work he abhorred. He scrupulously saved his money, retired early, drew a circle around his life that enclosed his wife and daughter, and constructed a routine in which to pass the remainder of his days.

This history, which I learned over the course of my growing up, now stands behind my recollection of my grandfather. It has become infused with my values and experiences, and it informs the way I recount my early love. As a result, what had charmed me about my grandfather's circumscribed existence now saddens me as an obvious effort to seal out memory and prevent further loss. His cautiousness and distrust of appearances, so reassuring and wise appearing to a small child, now bespeak fear and carry the imprint of profound disappointment. Even his intense love for me seems retrospectively freighted with the baggage of lost love—as though he were trying to recreate in our small alliance the easy camaraderie he had had with his siblings during his childhood in Russia.

Coming to see this as I grew, my own life developed in counterpoint to his. My impatience with routine must certainly have evolved in part to oppose the predictability and caution that I came to associate with his failure. In the same way Alice Walker's adult consciousness informs her writing. We hear it explicitly in the paragraph that summarizes the injustices Mr. Sweet suffered. But it is also implicit in the way the story is written—in its meticulous fund of detail and its disciplined structure. Walker, the accomplished professional writer, shows none of the irresponsibility and wastefulness that characterized Mr. Sweet. Lurking in both her story and mine is the sense that the old men we loved should have led different sorts of lives and that we, their successors, have tried to learn from their failure and to wrest from society and history what we feel they were deprived of. Our adult consciousness, unlike our child's consciousness, is judgmental and instrumental. It appraises, critiques, preaches, and acts.

At the same time, of course, our stories are wistful and nostalgic. They yearn to forget what experience has taught, to forget thinking and doing, and to give ourselves over to dancing and long walks. In this they suggest the sad possibility that what we love first may become the model for what we teach ourselves to reject—childhood loves being, by definition, suspect to the adult mind, which compartmentalizes, limits, and censures. Dickens grasped this most acutely and proceeded to idealize the children in his novels, with those who were most ideal consigned to early deaths, incapable of withstanding the crippling effects of experience.

Adult consciousness—the consciousness that Dickens parodied in his myriad of unbending schoolmasters—not only lacks charm but also, for all its access to reason and facts, for all its ability to get things done and even effect change, lacks the ability to satisfactorily explain the way things are. When I try to derive precise historical lessons from my grandfather's life, I find that I can only go so far. I might co-opt pieces for a given agenda of the moment, but I cannot make any satisfying sense of the whole unless I keep at a distance and content myself with generalizations. Part of the problem lies with the confused messages that he himself relayed during his lifetime, his almost perverse unwillingness to represent himself as a simple victim or as an object lesson of any sort. He had escaped the worst persecution in European history, and yet he tended to glorify the old days and to be irritated by things that were, as he put it, "modern." He was not flexible; he led a circumscribed life; yet he could be surprisingly tolerant and open with people and could cross barriers of difference with apparent ease. This had earned him a range of unlikely admirers, from the black janitor in his Brooklyn apartment building to the Jehovah's Witness who was surprised to have him listen to her with real attention, ask questions, and finally try to argue her out of her beliefs. He also had unlikely enemies—a number of elderly Jewish men whom he had alienated by defending the Communists (though with others he ardently condemned them) and with whom he seemed to take pride in not being on speaking terms.

But even more than the contradictory messages that get in the way of a coherent picture of my grandfather is the feeling, the legacy of that childhood bond, that he does not exist in history but in imagination. That he had views on this or that was nothing to me as a child—his Russian past was a fairy tale; I never associated it with real suffering or loss. It amused me to think that he would intimidate and infuriate others, and I used to giggle with him when one of his neighbors passed without saying hello. His stubbornesses and bitter pronouncements were to me strawmen in the way of my ability to get him to laugh and adore me.

Alice Walker's story is similar in that, despite the reference to Mr. Sweet's obstacles, it doesn't dwell on them; the story takes hold as it registers the success of Mr. Sweet's life in the consciousness of the child, and, as such, it escapes even as it records the coordinates of poverty and discrimination of black people in the South during the 1950s. It becomes exchangeable with any child's love for something or someone at any time or place. Indeed, this escape from history and society that the story records is what makes it possible for me to identify with it so intensely.

When at the end of her story the narrator is called home from college to once again revive Mr. Sweet, she makes clear that confidence in her own saving power is gone. Circulating in the adult world of books and ideas, up north in a society in which she has come to self-consciously see herself as a black woman and has begun to arm herself as one, she is no longer the powerful innocent capable of reviving the old man.

One of Henry James's late novels, *What Maisie Knew,* is the story of a little girl, shuttled among a group of selfish and opportunistic adults, whose child's consciousness puts only the most generous construction on what goes on. James refers in his preface to the "death" of Maisie's childhood as marking the close of the book—this is territory that he has chosen not to explore. Walker's brief tale, in this sense, goes further than James's. It records the effects of the passage from innocence to experience. Once her narrator ceases being a child, she is no longer able to magically sustain Mr. Sweet. That last visit home ends with the old man's death.

During the summer after my freshman year in college my grandfather suffered chest pain and was admitted to the local hospital for a workup. While there, he developed pneumonia and was forced to stay longer than expected. I remember visiting him in his room one evening, watching him sign checks and put his papers in order. He performed this work with his usual care and methodicalness. He was very busy and not depressed, yet I sensed something strange and charged in our meeting. I kissed and hugged him—I have a special recollection of whining for him to smile—and didn't leave until he had promised me that he would be fine. But the next day when I stopped at the hospital, I saw a crowd of doctors in front of the room and was held back near the nurses' station. They were trying to revive him but were unsuccessful. His heart had stopped. I was permitted to see him after they had given up, lying quietly, his eyes closed. I kissed him, but there was no getting him to smile again.

Walker's story recalls to me the complex emotions that accompanied my last visit. She is able to conflate the sense of Mr. Sweet's growing older with the passing of the narrator's childhood and to show them to be interlocking events. Implicitly, she raises the question: Had the narrator been able to remain in her childhood world (not gone off to Massachusetts, not educated herself away from her roots), might she have been able to revive Mr. Sweet? She captures the sense one feels that choices get made in growing up that preclude the realization of former hopes and earlier loves. Yet, instead of ending on this note—the note of betrayal and loss, of the road not taken—the story ends more positively, with the passing on of the old man's guitar to the narrator: "He had asked them months before to give it to me; he had known that even if I came next time he would not be able to respond in the old way.

He did not want me to feel that my trip had been for nothing." This gift is doubly suggestive: it asserts a level of control and knowingness in the old man (implying that he knew, perhaps decided, that this time he was going to die), and it symbolizes the bequeathing of a voice to the narrator. This voice is expressed in the telling of the story—a story that both mimics Mr. Sweet in its lyrical eloquence and frames him in its political awareness.

In her collection of essays *In Search of Our Mothers' Gardens* Walker expresses the mixed nature of her response to her past in what could serve as explicit commentary on her story of Mr. Sweet: "I [do not] intend to romanticize the Southern black country life," she writes.

> The hard work in the fields, the shabby houses, the evil greedy men who worked my father to death and almost broke the courage of that strong woman, my mother. No, I am simply saying that Southern black writers, like most writers, have a heritage of love and hate, but that they also have enormous richness and beauty to draw from. And, having been placed, as Camus says, "halfway between misery and the sun," they, too, know that "though all is not well under the sun, history is not everything."

When I visited my grandfather in the hospital the night before he died, my mind was on other things—on some boy from Indiana whom I had met during my freshman year and on the courses I would be taking in the fall. He was no longer central to my life, and so I link his dying to my distractedness and continue to feel that I had the power to kill him as I had the power to keep him alive. I can see this now as a still-childish delusion and realize that he was old and that my grandmother's illness had drained him and removed much of the supporting structure of his life—indeed, I now can see that her concrete ministrations, far more than my magical ones, had kept him alive. Yet the feeling of power my grandfather engendered in me is not one I ever want to let go of entirely. I associate it with the gift of the guitar in the Walker story— and I often feel that when I write I am convincing myself, as I thought I was convincing him, that orderliness, happiness, and life will prevail.

Sisters

W HEN, in 1929, Virginia Woolf surveyed the quality of women's writing in the nineteenth century, she focused on the problem of style: "the first thing [a female writer] would find, setting pen to paper, was that there was no common sentence ready for her use." The "common sentence"—the rhetorical currency that serves as the literary foundation of a culture—was, according to Woolf, "a man's sentence": with it Charlotte Brontë "stumbled and fell," and George Eliot "committed atrocities." The exception, she said, was Jane Austen. Of the female writers of the nineteenth century only Austen saw no obstacle in the sentence bequeathed to her: "Jane Austen looked at it and laughed at it and devised a perfectly natural, shapely sentence proper for her own use and never departed from it."

Against this admiring assessment of Jane Austen's style, now consider another assessment, one that was first given wide circulation by the respected literary critic Marvin Mudrick in his 1952 book, *Jane Austen: Irony as Defense and Discovery*. Mudrick argues that Austen's distinctive ironic style, while it provided her with perspective on her subject, was also her defense against the kinds of emotional entanglements that she depicted in her novels. Hers, Mudrick concludes, was a "hard compelled detachment." The critic John Halperin, in his 1984 biography of Jane Austen, takes up where Mudrick leaves off and arrives at even more extreme conclusions. Halperin finds "bitter irony" in *Northanger Abbey* and "blackness" in *Sense and Sensibility*, a novel that, he maintains, is "prevented from being truly great by the author's ill-temper and impatience with her own characters." Austen's unfinished mid-career novel, *The Watsons*, he says, reflects "the frustration, despair, and loneliness of Jane Austen's barren middle years," while *Mansfield Park* is "her most unpleasant novel," made worse by "another botched ending." By the time Halperin arrives at Austen's last novel, *Persuasion*, he is indignant: "gratuitously harsh, shockingly cruel and malicious," he intones of one satirical passage in this novel, "only a woman deficient in feeling and, yes, 'taste,' could have written it."

What are we to conclude about Austen's style? Halperin reads in Austen's easy hand with irony and summary statement, the repression, bitterness, and despair of an unhappy spinster. Virginia Woolf reads in the same stylistic tendencies a blithe disregard for the common sentence of the age and the mastery of a perfectly unconflicted personal voice. Are we dealing with a misreading on one side or the other?

In a review of Halperin's biography that I wrote after it came out, I accused him of just such a misreading. Clearly, I argued, this man disliked Jane Austen and had no business writing about her. He seemed to me stone deaf when it came to her satire and unduly concerned with matters of sensitivity and taste. One might have taken him for a spurned lover, not a biographer. But I have since changed my view of what constitutes an acceptable perspective for a literary critic. I have become convinced that how we read is contingent upon many personal variables; that all readings are, in some way, idiosyncratic; and that the best we can do is give an honest reading according to our own nature. Far from arguing that Halperin has no business writing Austen's biography, I now acknowledge that he has provided an especially consistent and useful *perspective* on Jane Austen (what is she, after all, but a convergence of perspectives?). Moreover, I now perceive that Halperin's hostility toward Austen is entwined with his fascination for her (the image of the lover is not so inappropriate). And, if his hostility feeds his fascination, it is at least a mode of access for him to a feminine world to which he might otherwise remain simply indifferent. By the same token I comprehend Virginia Woolf's admiration for Austen somewhat differently now. It is a less simple thing than I previously imagined, containing its share of envy and hostility. If Halperin's reading offers insight into some of the less explored aspects of male-female relations, Woolf's reveals some of the finer contradictions that can enter into one woman's perspective on another.

We can begin to gain an understanding of the effect of Jane Austen's style on a reader like Halperin, if we examine a key scene from *Pride and Prejudice*, certainly her most popular and arguably her most stylistically representative novel. The scene is the Meryton Ball, at which Austen has assembled her characters for the purpose of launching her romantic plot. As we gain access to the scene, the ball has been in progress for some time, and we are informed that Elizabeth Bennet, our heroine, "had been obliged, by the scarcity of partners, to sit down for two dances." Fortunately, she is seated so as to overhear an exchange between two gentlemen standing nearby. John Bingley, a wealthy bachelor already smitten with Elizabeth's pretty sister Jane, has been urging his aristocratic friend Darcy to ask Elizabeth to dance:

> "Which do you mean?" [Darcy replies] and turning round, he looked for a moment at Elizabeth, till catching her eye he withdrew his own and coldly said, "She is tolerable; but not handsome enought to tempt *me*; and I am in no humour at present to give consequence to young ladies who are slighted by other men."

How Elizabeth responds to these unflattering words is all-important: it will determine everything that follows. She does not hide and brood over the offense; she recounts it "with great spirit among her friends; for she had a lively, playful disposition, which delighted in any thing ridiculous." By publicizing Darcy's remark and doing so in a spirit of satire, she converts her vulnerability into a source of power. When, on a subsequent occasion, Darcy does ask her to dance, she returns the original snub with a definiteness and confidence that now seem to make inevitable his pursuit of her.

I would suggest that John Halperin experiences the same kind of maneuvering at the hands of Jane Austen that Darcy experiences at the hands of Elizabeth Bennet. Darcy struggles against loving Elizabeth—his will and better judgment are against it—but he is nonetheless seduced, as he admits in the end, by her "impertinence" (itself a reaction to his own impertinence, though he doesn't know it). In a similar fashion Halperin seems drawn to Austen's work for the very qualities that offend him (lapses of taste, failures of sensitivity), themselves arguably the response to male offenses against women built into the literary (and cultural) tradition. If Halperin finds much to fault in Austen's style, he has also taken the time to read and reread, write and rewrite on the subject—to make a career, in short, of his disapproval. If that doesn't sound like a marriage, I don't know what does.

But let me pursue the analogy I have attempted to draw between the two couples: Darcy and Elizabeth, Halperin and Austen. I have suggested that the appeal of Elizabeth Bennet to Darcy is grounded in the game of playing hard to get. But such a game is only practical in a fic-

tional setting. Austen admits as much when she has Darcy find Elizabeth's impertinence so surprising: he has never experienced it from a
woman before. In other words, in real life (at least during Jane Austen's
day) women did not behave this way. They hadn't the luxury of
indulging their wit in a society in which getting a husband was considered the only road to satisfaction and support for a woman. And
doesn't the same hold for the female writer of the period? Given a masculine literary tradition, how can she risk an impertinent style? Male
satirists have traditionally defined themselves as isolated beings (one
thinks of Jonathan Swift or Molière's Alceste), but there have been few
female satirists for the reason that women simply haven't had the societal support to sustain a satirical voice in isolation. Halperin's critique
of Austen's insensitivity and bad taste shows that notions of feminine
propriety still exist to hamper a woman with a gift for satire. Elizabeth
Bennet can indulge her wit "like a man" without much need of external
verification because she has the confidence of her creator: Austen
stacks the deck in her favor. But where did Austen herself gain the confidence of her distinctive style? Who stacked the deck for her?

The key to the mystery happens to be right there on page 184 of
Halperin's biography. He writes, "Jane and Cassandra shared a bedroom, as they always had done." From the time of her juvenilia Jane
had retreated with her sister, Cassandra, to their shared bedroom for
readings of her work in progress (preludes to the more formal readings
of finished works that were given to the family as a whole). Relatives
recall the peals of laughter that emanated from that room. In noting
that the arrangement of a shared bedroom would be continued,
Halperin is referring to the women's move in 1809 to Chawton Cottage,
part of a property owned by their brother Edward. Only a few pages
earlier he had told us that the cottage was no cottage really but, rather,
a large house with six bedrooms. The occupants were Jane, Cassandra,
and their mother, with periodic visits from a stray nephew or niece. In
short, there was no need for Jane and Cassandra, now well into their
thirties, to continue to share a bedroom. But they did. That room, I suggest, was the symbolic site of Jane Austen's stylistic development—a
development born out of sisterly complicity. Austen faced the sentence
bequeathed to her by a masculine literary tradition and dismissed it for
one of her own because she always had her sister there for her. "My

dearest Cassandra," writes Jane in 1813, "Your letter was truly welcome, and I am much obliged to you for all your praise; it came at a right time, for I had had some fits of disgust. Our second evening's reading [of *Pride and Prejudice*] to Miss Benn had not pleased me so well."

Jane's allusion to Cassandra's "praise" may put us in mind of the support that the philosopher and critic George Henry Lewes provided to a later nineteenth-century female novelist, George Eliot. In fact, it is different. Lewes's job was to shield Eliot, whose sense of self-doubt was profound and abiding, always threatening to intrude, destroy her peace, and stall her work. This was not Jane Austen's problem. Self-doubt had never paralyzed her. Her reference to "fits of disgust" with *Pride and Prejudice* seems like a throwaway, full of cavalier exaggeration, for in the next breath she has admitted that "upon the whole . . . I am quite vain enough and well satisfied enough." Since Jane had always had an essentially sympathetic audience in her sister, she had no need that this audience be slavish in its support. She could encourage herself when the occasion warranted, and thus it seems she depended upon Cassandra more for control (both emotional and literary) than for reinforcement. In thanking her sister for quelling her disgust, one senses that she is acknowledging not her own insecurity so much as her sister's critical contributions, her gift for pragmatic revision. Cassandra, in other words, could not only subdue fits of disgust but also prune an overwritten scene and an overdrawn portrait. Jane says as much in her 1813 letter to Cassandra when she notes her own wish to stretch out a novel with material "unconnected with the story" and then anticipates her sister's reaction: "I doubt your quite agreeing with me here. I know your starched notions." When an Austen niece, an aspiring novelist herself, sent a manuscript to her aunts for comment, Jane would reply: "Your Aunt C. does not like desultory novels, & is rather afraid yours will be too much so. . . . It will not be so great an objection to me if it does." Given the tightly plotted nature of Austen's novels, we can assume that Cassandra helped rid them of much "desultory" matter. We know that she performed the editorial role in one instance at least. To the dismay of future biographers, she did a devastatingly complete job editing her sister's correspondence after her death.

But I will press this notion of Cassandra's editorial contribution still further. I will argue that the distinctive style that we associate with Jane Austen's novels derived from a complementarity of manner and judgment in Jane and Cassandra that was contained and nurtured within the safe harbor of their sisterly relationship. It was a complementarity grown out of those "happy hours of confidential intercourse" (Cassandra's words) that passed behind the door of their shared bedroom. We glimpse the shadow of this collaboration in the mutually supportive yet opposing roles of Elinor and Marianne Dashwood in *Sense and Sensibility* and of Elizabeth and Jane Bennet in *Pride and Prejudice*. In both novels one sister is designated as the talker and the other as the listener, but, since in one case the heroine is the listener and in the other the talker, we must, it seems to me, view the sisters' interaction as one in which there is no simple hierarchy and in which the creative contribution cannot be localized in one or the other role.

We also gain insight into the sisterly dynamic in Jane Austen's letters, in which Cassandra is represented as the more disciplined and careful writer ("Your close-written letter makes me quite ashamed of my wide lines"), the better authority on aesthetic matters ("I have . . . changed the trimmings of my cap this morning; they are now such as you suggested"), and the more "tender-hearted." There is neither jealousy nor undue awe in Jane's references to Cassandra's "qualities"; they are delivered with that affectionate irony that designates them a part of family lore. Sisterly complementarity was no doubt a reflexive aspect of Jane and Cassandra's relationship while also being embedded in that larger sense of agreement, that recognition of mutual need, that we associate with the exchange of form and content and of imagination and convention as these elements are said to operate in the creation of a work of art.

Yet my claim that the novels achieve their power through a creative but highly formalized sisterly dynamic must ultimately find support in more unorthodox forms of evidence. To stitch together such a thesis I step outside of my subject and inside of myself, for I bring to bear evidence whose source lies in my personal response to Austen's style. The truth is that when I read *Pride and Prejudice* I hear the sister's wrangling in the background. I hear Cassandra arguing that Charlotte Lucas's portrait be softened against Jane's inclination to be more severe, and I hear Cassandra suggesting touches (as she did with their hats)—that

Miss Anne de Bourgh, for example (the girl Darcy is supposed to marry), be a poor eater and have a screen to shield her weak eyes during the famous gathering at Rosings . . .

> "A screen! That's it," shrieks Jane, "and she'll have that bony, round-shouldered look, like S—— at the pump room in Bath last year . . . !"
> "Don't overdraw, Jane, keep her in the background now. Even with Miss Bingley, I think you may have overdone . . ."

When I read Austen's novels I hear these voices—and they are familiar—because they echo the voices of my sister and me at work on some collaborative project of our childhood. Unlike Halperin or even Woolf (a woman and a sister but not a complicitous sister, as I shall argue), I lay claim to an insider's comprehension of Austen, despite differences in historical period, social class, nationality, religion, and a million other things. For I intuit the same kind of complicity between Jane and Cassandra that I shared with my own sister. This sisterly complicity, I contend, lies at the heart of Austen's style: it is central to the development of that rhetorical ease with which she hits her target in apparent disregard for obstacles and detractors.

My sister and I grew up in the 1960s in a three-bedroom split-level in the New Jersey suburbs. We were a far cry from the Steventon Rectory, but in one thing we resembled the Austen girls: we shared a bedroom from as far back as I can remember. How can I express to those who haven't been there the safety and fun of that room—how completely it sheltered us from the difficulties of growing up and of being girls? In it we fine-tuned our sisterhood, taking what native intelligence and personal gifts we had and finding an admiring mirror for them in each other. Our relationship protected us from the violence of our adolescent emotions and the pain of disappointment. It entertained us and gave us confidence. Perhaps we weren't as clever and original as we thought we were, but that hardly mattered since we had each other to think so, and with that confidence we convinced others.

My sister and I existed during our growing up in a complex symbiosis. Although the younger-older distinction always held for us to some extent—I was my sister's protector, she was my docile playmate—this simple hierarchy took on nuances and shifts, as her position also became the site of freer imaginative forays to my more conventional point of view (Emma to my Harriet), of more volatile emotional displays to my greater self-control (Marianne to my Elinor), and of wittier, more lacerating judgments to my more generous assessments (Elizabeth to my Jane). Our position with respect to heroinism continually flip-flopped, for we negotiated a system of relative authorities that satisfied us both.

It is difficult to say whether we will ever quite recover from the disturbance of that sisterly ecology. That it was disturbed was a function of modern life. We were separated by college and career, and this, in turn, made possible the more complete separation produced through the acquiring of husbands and children. Had not circumstances divided us, I imagine that my sister and I would still be sharing a bedroom, turning over the days' activities like practiced collectors, transforming everyone around us into props for our amusement, and being cast as heroines in each other's dramas. If we were fortunate in having escaped the confinement of such a life, it is at the price of never again feeling so clever and so right. When I search for a deft phrase that doesn't come or when I look for the confidence that will sweep away doubt in a decision or a judgment, I know that some essential power relating to style has been lost by the severing of that connection.

For the Austen sisters there was the brief moment when this outcome might have been theirs. Cassandra became engaged in 1792, and, had her fiancé not died of yellow fever in the West Indies, one wonders what would have become of Jane. Perhaps she would have married, too—accepting one of the proposals that it is speculated she received—and thereby had her "delicious play of Mind . . . all settled down into conjugal & maternal affections," as she jokingly predicted would be the case for her favorite niece, Fanny Knight. More probably, had Cassandra married, the superficial events of Jane's life would not have changed appreciatively, but her confidence would have left her. She would have become a querulous old maid of the type she imagined in the character of *Emma*'s Miss Bates. Her style would have failed to sustain its authority; the sentence that she found for herself would have been lost. I doubt, indeed, that she would have been able to write, as she did in a letter addressed to her sister on the occasion of a ball in

1808 (by then she was thirty-three and Cassandra, thirty-five): "It was the same room in which we danced 15 years ago!—I thought it all over—& in spite of the shame of being so much older, felt with thankfulness that I was quite as happy now as then."

Rachel M. Brownstein, in her book *Becoming a Heroine: Reading about Women in Novels,* has also noted the importance of the sisterly relationship for Jane Austen. But she focuses on the rivalry inherent in that relationship. As evidence for that rivalry, she quotes from the letters: "How do you do to-day? [writes Jane to Cassandra in 1801] I hope you improve in sleeping—I think you must, because *I* fall off; I have been awake ever since five and sooner." Here is a world, explains Brownstein, in which one sister's loss is another's gain. But surely such a verdict ignores the satirical tone of the remark that takes advantage of rivalry but converts it to satire—removing its sting. "I am still without silk," Jane writes to Cassandra on another occasion, "You must get me some in town or in Canterbury; it should be finer than yours." This is not rivalry; it is a parody of rivalry. In adopting a satirical tone Jane places Cassandra and herself in an equal position of detachment with respect to the thing being satirized: there can now be no greater gain or loss involved for either. In short, the rivalry inherent in their relationship is converted to give energy and edge to the position of detachment: it is deflected from each other and directed outward toward the world.

By the same token one can understand why Austen was such a severe critic of sentimentality in her novels. Sentimentality is what satire fears it will be if it stops turning rivalry to constructive use and takes refuge in artificial agreement. One of the few instances in the letters in which Jane Austen's style seems forced and stilted occurs when she writes to her sister on the death of their brother's wife: "Edward's loss is terrible, and must be felt as such, and these are too early days indeed to think of moderation in grief, either in him or his afflicted daughter." So ill adapted is she to the sentimental style that her writing in this letter of condolence seems to read at times like her own parodies of sentiment ("I suppose you see the corpse? How does it appear?" and "I am to be in bombazeen and crape, according to what we are told is universal here"). Only as she begins to consciously relax into her old satirical voice does the writing regain its ease and fluency. "I hope your sorrowing party were at church yesterday, and have no longer *that* to dread," she writes a week later. The letters demonstrate how completely wedded Austen was to satire as a mode of addressing her sister. It is hardly surprising that no letters regarding Cassandra's engagement or the death of her fiancé—indeed, no serious discussion of an attachment, a disappointment, or a loss of any kind—exists (with the exception of the one case already mentioned and of the truly moving but notably restrained letter written by Cassandra to her niece on the occasion of Jane's death). Such feelings either were never expressed in the letters or were edited out for the reason that they "rang wrong" to the sisters. Jane and Cassandra had worked too hard forging a style in which they felt safe and powerful not to be rattled when one of them hit the wrong note.

If rivalry is converted to satire in Austen's writing to her sister, it emerges, its fangs intact, in Virginia Woolf's writing on Austen. I have cited Woolf's unreserved praise of Austen's style, but there is a price exacted for such praise. It comes in the form of an attack on another front:

> for my own part [Woolf writes of Austen in her essay "Personalities"], I would rather not find myself alone in the room with her. A sense of meaning withheld, a smile at something unseen, an atmosphere of perfect control and courtesy mixed with something finely satirical, which, were it not directed against things in general rather than against individuals, would be almost malicious, would, so I feel, make it alarming to find her at home.

Unsurprisingly, Halperin cites this passage as a shrewd observation on Woolf's part. It reflects the place at which their two perspectives on Austen meet. But there is a bitter wistfulness to Woolf's passage, which Halperin fails to discern. If, as a man, Halperin senses he is being laughed at by Jane Austen, as a woman, Virginia Woolf feels excluded—feels that she has missed something. What she wouldn't give, I read beneath the surface of Woolf's portrait, to share in that smile, to see the unseen, to be at home with Jane. To be, in short, in the privileged position of Cassandra! "She flatters and cajoles you with the promise of intimacy," writes Woolf of Austen earlier in the same essay,

"and then, at the last moment, there is the same blankness." The tone
here is of a shy girl contemplating a desired but inaccessible playmate.
Virginia Woolf was drawn to women throughout her lifetime, and
these relationships often took obsessive forms. According to one biographer, her tie to her sister, Vanessa, and to her half-sister, Stella
(whose death prompted her first major nervous collapse), resembled
these later friendships in being "a mix of chivalric crush and immature
clinging"—not at all the kind of thing likely to give rise to creative collaboration. Moreover, none of these relationships was without its share
of palpable friction and antagonism. It would seem that the rivalry
inherent in her relationship with her sisters and with women in general
never underwent the kind of transformation that Jane and Cassandra
were able to achieve through satire. Perhaps Woolf's development as a
serious novelist concerned with the interior life of the individual grew
out of something intractably autonomous in her nature, but, if so, the
conditions and the temperament that made sisterly complicity impossible for her may also be connected to that pervasive loneliness, that
sense of cosmic solitude, that would plague her throughout her life and
contribute to her tragic death. Woolf argued that female writers need a
room of their own in order to create great literature, but I think she
secretly wished she could share one—that she envied Jane Austen both
the ease and confidence of her style and the sisterly complicity that lay
behind it.

The older I grow and the further away I am from sisterly complicity, the more I am attracted to the beautifully crafted qualifications and
subtle ironies of Virginia Woolf. But it is in my distance from the certainty and confidence I once felt when my sister's ear and voice were
never far off that this appreciation has sprung. No doubt, Jane and Cassandra, safe in the unassailable fortress of their relationship, would
have had no patience with Virginia Woolf's portentous run-ons, her
preoccupation with interior life, or her ambivalence. "Get to the point,"
they would have said. "Don't preach so much about men's vanity; caricature the ones who snubbed you. Make us laugh."

At one point in his biography John Halperin cites an earlier male critic
who described Jane Austen as "plump, prim, and pop-eyed" in the
famous portrait of her by Cassandra. The quote not only impugns
Jane's looks but also Cassandra's motives, for it insinuates that some

kind of hostility or rivalry played a role in the way she portrayed her sister. The inclusion of the quote seems gratuitous. I interpret it to reflect Halperin's desire to cast aspersions on Austen and on that sisterly relationship; I see it reflecting his defensiveness concerning his own imagined status in the eyes of his subject. Yet for all his apparent reservations and disapprovals John Halperin has written a biography of Jane Austen much as Darcy was drawn against his will to propose to Elizabeth Bennet. He is, I suspect, half in love with that pop-eyed girl, though I doubt he would have had the nerve to effect an introduction had the opportunity presented itself.

"There was one gentleman," Jane wrote to Cassandra in 1799 on the subject of a recent ball, "an officer of the Cheshire, a very good-looking young man, who, I was told, wanted very much to be introduced to me; but as he did not want it quite enough to take much trouble in effecting it, we never could bring it about." Like Elizabeth Bennet, Jane Austen has turned herself from a wallflower into a powerful satirical observer. But, while the novel heroine used her wit to win her a husband, Austen's wit, as it finds an audience and an echo in her sister, is its own reward.

Turning the Screw on Dr. Spock

*C*HE other day, when I picked my son up from his day care center, he was in the sullen mood that tells me something has happened to upset him. On the way home I asked him what was wrong, and, after some prodding, he confessed that his teacher, Miss Diane, had been "mad" at him that day.

"Why was Miss Diane mad at you?"
"Because I used filthy language."
"What's filthy language?"
"I don't know."
"Well, what words did you say that made her mad?"
"'Underpants.'"
"Is that all?"
(*Thinks*) "Maybe 'pupy'" (a nonspecific word for genitals used in our family), "and 'penis.'"
"Why did you say those words?"
"I don't know."
"Miss Diane doesn't think those are polite words, so don't say them anymore around her, okay?"
"Okay."
"It's okay to say those words around Mommy, but not around Miss Diane, okay?"
"Okay."
"Would you like Mommy to get you a book that explains about the difference between boys and girls?"
(*Enthusiastically*) "Yeah." (*Pause*) "Can I have ice cream?"

This conversation resembles others Sam and I have had during his two years in full-time day care. It reflects an effort on my part to do a number of things at once: to elicit information, to reinforce the authoritative pronouncements of his teacher, to correct or revise those pronouncements, and to address what I believe was the original concern in my child's mind that triggered the incident—all this without seeming to give too much importance to the whole thing. The result is a web of precepts, counterprecepts, and interventions, delicately suspended in an air of casualness, which I hope will give my son what he needs while leaving him open to new experience—will direct his development without oppressing him.

The delicacy, however, with which I approach situations like the one I just described also has more complex motives behind it—motives that I suspect other parents of my generation harbor. My willingness to accommodate the views of Miss Diane is more than a pragmatic response to norms with which I disagree but that I feel my child must respect. It also reflects my own methodological doubts. I am not convinced that Miss Diane's approach will hurt my child any more than that my approach will help or, indeed, that our approaches will necessarily have different effects. I know that by prodding my son for information, by asking leading questions, and by suggesting a particular kind of book, I am beginning a process whose outcome I feel helpless to predict. Suspecting this, my interventions tend necessarily to be tentative, qualified, and rarely simple. In the conversation I have recorded here, my son's request for ice cream stands out poignantly for me. In it I seem to hear the natural boy struggling to free himself from my attempt at intervention.

What is the relationship between nature and nurture? What should socialization consist of, and how should it be carried out? These are the questions that parents wrestle with today more self-consciously than ever before. I have mentioned a concern for openness and naturalness. These values are the legacy of Dr. Spock and a more innocent age; as so-called enlightened parents, we continue to use them, but without the conviction of our parents. We have begun to question whether they are constructive values or destructive ones: the basis for our best selves or the source of a social anarchy that may now be threatening our ability to live orderly lives. We are also more skeptical about how natural our ideas about nature really are. My son's plea for ice cream seems natural to me in the context of our conversation, but, on reconsideration, I wonder whether this may be his wily way of taking advantage of a situation in which he senses I am vulnerable. Thus, the notion of what is natural recedes as we think to grasp it. Our fate as contemporary parents is to be painfully aware that we are working according to a makeshift model, one that is bound to change with the next edition of Dr. Spock's *Baby and Child Care.*

In a society in which all values have been called into question, in which even the most liberal authorities have come to seem arbitrary and coercive, where can we go for guidance? It seems to me that in the climate of skepticism that pervades contemporary culture, our help as parents lies not in prescriptive manuals but in imaginative literature— in texts that we would never have dreamed of consulting for guidance during a less ambivalent age. One such text is Henry James's famous ghost story and masterpiece of psychological fiction, *The Turn of the Screw.* Written in 1898, when James was entering the last and most self-reflexive phase of his career, the story is both a cautionary tale and a profound expression of sympathy for the zealous parent. Its insights are especially illuminating given the kinds of dilemmas facing contemporary parents.

The Turn of the Screw is told from the point of view of a young governess who is retained to care for the orphaned niece and nephew of a wealthy London bachelor. Her employer makes only one stipulation when he hires her: that she take full responsibility for the children at his country estate while he be left undisturbed to carry on his life in town.

When the governess arrives at her post she is dazzled by the beauty and seeming pliability of the children. But she also experiences strange premonitions and forebodings, especially when she discovers that the boy, despite his angelic appearance, has been expelled from his school for unspecified reasons. Not long after this discovery, she has a series of eerie encounters on the grounds of the estate—first, with a mysterious man and, later, with an equally mysterious woman. These she eventually identifies as the ghosts of her employer's former valet, Peter Quint, and of the children's former governess, Miss Jessel (believed to be Quint's lover), both of whom had died shortly before her arrival. She becomes convinced that the ghosts have come for the children, and she determines to thwart them. Although she fails to gain the confidence of the little girl who, when confronted, accuses her of being insane, the boy proves more tractable. He begins to confess to seemingly minor, but to the governess highly significant, acts of misconduct, among them that he was thrown out of school for "saying things"

("things," the governess deduces, taught him by the evil Quint). In the story's climactic scene she seeks to exorcise the ghost's influence from the boy and succeeds in doing so, only to have him die in the process.

So skillfully is the story constructed from the governess's point of view that it wasn't until 1934, when Freudian psychology began to become popular in literary circles, that the eminent critic Edmund Wilson proposed an interpretation challenging the reality of the ghosts. Wilson argued that James's story was a tale not of the supernatural but of the unconscious and that the ghosts were fantasies resulting from the governess's sexual repressions (a diagnosis that curiously resembles that of the little girl in the story). "We now see," Wilson declares with the kind of insistence that recalls the governess's certainty about the ghosts, "that [the story] is a variation on one of James's familiar themes: the frustrated Anglo-Saxon spinster." It is an index to how thoroughly the notion of repression has been made a culprit for society's ills that Wilson's Freudian perspective has now been almost universally adopted as the "meaning" of *The Turn of the Screw*. But, while this reading has the virtue of recognizing the psychological dimension to James's story that had formerly been ignored, its narrow focus on the governess's sexual neuroses is as reductive as the literalist reading that preceded it. We need to widen our perspective if we are to grasp the story's relevance to contemporary readers and, in particular, its insights into the difficulties inherent in child rearing.

As parents, it seems to me that we have a good deal in common with the governess in *The Turn of the Screw*. Like her, we often seem bent upon counteracting influences from "outside" as they touch our children in what we take to be false or corrupting ways. At the same time, we also harbor an awareness that the pernicious influences may well be our own—or that we may contribute to impressing those influences on our children even as we seek to combat them. Ours is the double bind of being at once our children's protectors and their corruptors, with no access to a third position. For we cannot abstain from influence either. Any attempt at withdrawal becomes its own form of emphasis or becomes an addition to a conspiracy of silence.

The governess's behavior can be understood as a naive attempt to grapple with this paradox of influence. In accepting her post early in the story, she is at first flattered by the confidence of her employer. She begins to grow uneasy, however, when faced with the actual children, "the vision of whose angelic beauty [she confesses to herself during her first night at her post] had probably more than anything else to do with the restlessness that . . . made me several times rise and wander about my room." The apparent perfection of the children is what disturbs her sleep. If they are as perfect as they seem, then all influence, including her own, is bound to be detrimental. In representing her role at this point in the story, the image she invokes is one of powerlessness: "I had the fancy of our being almost as lost as a handful of passengers in a great drifting ship. Well, I was, strangely, at the helm!" Significantly, however, the ghosts appear to her soon afterward, and this precipitates a change in the way she conceives her role: "We were united in our danger [she reflects now of herself and the children]. . . . I was a screen—I was to stand before them." The presence of a third element, the ghosts, "unites" her with the children and gives her her cue, fixing her in opposition to "danger." And herein lies her help. For if the process of the children's social development has already been started before her arrival—and started in the wrong direction—then her own job becomes easier (more technically difficult perhaps but less morally daunting). Even if she destroys the children in the process of caring for them, she can now rationalize this outcome as an improvement over what might have been had the forces of evil been permitted to triumph.

Most parents are unable to produce such unambiguous threats to their children as the governess is able to discover for herself in *The Turn of the Screw*. But there are exceptions. A nasty divorce can sometimes turn the person of the former spouse into something as good—or, rather, as bad—as a Miss Jessel or a Peter Quint. Take the much publicized case of Dr. Elizabeth Morgan, an Ivy League–trained physician who accused her ex-husband of sexually molesting their daughter. When the judge in the case ruled that insufficient evidence existed to support her claim and that the child's visitation with the father should continue, Dr. Morgan had her daughter placed in hiding and proceeded to go to prison for defying a court order. If the facts of the case were ambiguous, one thing appeared certain: Elizabeth Morgan believed she was saving her daughter from a monstrous father and a complicitous judge. By positioning herself in opposition to what she saw to be evil, she was able to exhibit a martyrlike resistance.

Although there have been other examples of such resistance (whole communities whipped into a frenzy over the presumed degeneracy of day-care center workers), the witch-hunt mentality exhibited by the plaintiffs in these cases is not representative of public sentiment in general. Most of us, it seems to me, are ready to acquit rather than condemn, as the judges and juries have tended to do. For one thing, working parents depend upon the services of nannies and day care workers in order to carry on their lives, and it is hard to condemn those upon whom one depends. Furthermore, we know that, if these people are damaging our children, they are doing so, for the most part, unintentionally. Indeed, they, more than we, are the obvious counterparts to the governess in James's story. On the day after the conversation with my son, his teacher took me aside, her lips pursed in disapproval, to comment that she had never heard such language out of the mouth of a four-year-old. Her words had me divided between two reactions: my sense of the foolishness of this woman's notion of bad language and my recognition that the language my son was using reflected badly on us, his parents. If, from the perspective of my husband and me, Miss Diane haunts our son, from her perspective, it is *we* who haunt him, and she is working quite as diligently to counteract our influence as we are working to counteract hers.

The fact is that, unlike the governess who may unconsciously invent her demons, I admit to the conscious creation of mine and therefore can't believe in their villainy or my own innocence quite as much. I know that I need the friction, mistakes, and stupidities of day care upon which to build my own philosophy. Moreover, even as I struggle to shape a method, I know that the possibility of coherent influence is itself the illusion, like ideas about nature and freedom. A child is never a blank slate. He or she comes not only with particular genetic characteristics already inscribed but also with an inherent susceptibility to stimuli whose sources, intensities, and combinations are unpredictable. James seems to be suggesting this when early in the story he has the governess learn of the little boy's expulsion from school. Unable to deal with the possibility of random influence and the notion that the child may be already mired in the complexities of socialization, she imagines a demonic plot to explain his history. Although the situation, as she interprets it, will require strenuous, even death-defying action from her, it has the advantage of tidying up the muddle of influence and the unpredictability of human character. It smacks of the housekeeping mentality.

Which may also be why the governess's attitude reminds me of the attitude that prevailed during my own childhood in the 1950s and 1960s when the model mother was also the model housekeeper: Donna Reed in a neat shirtwaist and pearls. The mothers of that era shared with James's governess a sense of the linear, plotted aspects of human development, of the possibility of putting children's lives in order as they might arrange the toys in their rooms. My mother-in-law once confessed to me that, because the *Ladies Home Journal* featured "model" meals containing meat, two vegetables, and a potato, she had felt compelled to serve her family such a meal every night. She believed that to omit one of these requisite items could have traumatic effects on the future of her children. Like the governess, she saw herself fighting a malicious though invisible foe, one that required a scrupulous attention to detail and a disciplined regimen to keep at bay.

But if the governess was forced to invent a method in order to do battle, our mothers, in being bred to the housewifely ideal, were provided with one ready-made. In their book *For Her Own Good: 150 Years of the Experts' Advice to Women*, Barbara Ehrenreich and Deirdre English argue that what informed all child-rearing tactics applied over the last and the greater part of this century was the authority of science. Despite shifts in approach from behaviorism to permissiveness, the fundamental premise remained the same: "it was the task of science to translate seemingly incomprehensible childish behavior into a pattern of cues for the mother to follow." To our current, more skeptical viewpoint such cues seem to resemble the directives of certain fundamentalist religions, in which everything has meaning and finds support or antidote in elaborate prescriptions and protocols. Any method that depends on such cues now appears less scientific than superstitious— or perhaps we have begun to relegate science to the realm of superstition (after all, if the governess on her own could produce a fairly convincing system of belief, one that withstood critical assault until at least 1934, imagine what a whole civilization working in concert could do along the same lines?). Our mothers seem to have gotten the worst of the bargain. They were shut out from participating in building the system of belief that they were expected to adopt, but they were positioned to be held responsible for the results. Even the governess knew that, if you're designated to stay home with the children, you're going to have to shoulder the blame for what goes wrong—and something inevitably will. She covered herself by bringing in ghosts. Our mothers only thumbed more vigorously through their manuals.

As parents today, we find ourselves in the triple position of being the casualties, the critics, and the heirs of the scientific fundamentalism that so many of our mothers adopted without question. We exhibit both an intense seriousness about what lies before us and a profound skepticism about experts and general methods. This attitude—at once fervent and doubting—has given rise to a new view of childhood. Instead of revering childhood for its simplicity, naturalness, and purity, as past generations did, we tend to revere—and fear—childhood for the way it challenges our most basic notions about cause and effect, narrative continuity, and decipherable meaning. When, a generation ago, mothers got together in their coffee klatches, they discussed generalized treatments for colic, regimens for toilet training, and salvos for sibling rivalry. Today these problems have ceased to have generalizable solutions. There are as many treatments and regimens as there are pediatricians and babies; one must take into account a hundred contextual variables before choosing a given course of action, and, even then, who knows? All that my pediatrician, a nationally known expert on colic, felt able to proffer when I explained that my infant daughter writhed and fussed during feeding was the enigmatic comment: "That's just her."

The new perspective on childhood suggests a greater willingness to accept the individuality of each child, but it also reflects a pervasive pessimism about the ability of society to educate and socialize its children. The list of possible reasons for a child's fall into delinquency is now acknowledged to be very long: Is it that the child was adopted, the parents divorced, the mother burdened with a drug habit, the teacher distracted and overworked? Was it the pressure of peers, the influence of movies or television or Nintendo? We are faced with an army of Miss Jessels and Peter Quints, and a governess seeking to do battle for a child's soul would not know where to begin.

With so many potential demons to contend with, many of us

understandably fall back on temporary and tentative insights in raising our children. We are more qualified in our responses than our parents were, more willing to reverse ourselves, trying to grasp an essence and to shape an essence, refusing to place one before the other. This kind of approach has some of the hallmarks of artistic creation, which always finds its source in the particular and which also has a hard time separating instinct from skill, inspired content from formal design, negative capability from positive purpose. During the nineteenth century the Romantic poets revered childhood, but their tendency was to invoke it as a metaphor for imaginative life and for natural development. The particularity of Romantic art came not from actual children but from social and natural phenomena that had not yet shown the effect of routinized political corruption and a sustained neglect for the environment. During the nineteenth century and early in this century it may have been unnecessary for poets, novelists, and philosophers to explore the behavior of actual children, since the world outside still offered promise.

But, then, we can return to Henry James and find that he stands out as an exception. He may even speak more compellingly to the complexities of understanding and raising children than contemporary writers do, because his voice, coming from an earlier and seemingly simpler age, has the force of prophecy. In the decade in which he wrote *The Turn of the Screw* James wrote several novels in which children figure and which explore to varying degrees the vulnerabilities and the powerful imaginative life of the individual child. Although James himself never married or had children, his sensitivity to issues involving the development and rearing of children has to do, I suspect, with the family in which he was raised. James's father was a philosopher who made his children his occupation. His method of child rearing was an anti-method—a mangle of contradiction and qualification. He despised professionalism and conformity, but he valued achievement. His notion of education was ambitious but vague, his precepts as ambiguous as that of any contemporary parent. The results of this method are worth noting. His eldest son, William, after several nervous breakdowns and after embarking unsuccessfully on a career as an artist and a scientist, eventually became a world-renowned philosopher and a pioneer in the field of modern psychology. The second son, Henry, despite his own share of nervous complaints, went on to write some of the greatest novels of the age, become the most discerning and innovative of literary critics, and usher in the literary movement of modernism. The three other James children were less successful though no more symptom free. Alice, the Jameses' only daughter, was a lifelong invalid, suffering from a variety of psychosomatic illnesses, while the younger brothers, Robertson and Wilkinson, led restless lives, mixing in a series of failed entrepreneurial schemes: Wilky died young; Robertson became an alcoholic. Still, it must be said that these children all professed an abiding love for one another and for their parents. Ultimately, it is hard to pass judgment on James Sr.'s child-rearing methods: one cannot trace the influences that helped to produce great achievement any more than those that went into the making of great suffering. What James Sr. did do was introduce his children to a philosophy of life that would become the basis for many of William James's philosophical principles and the central core of Henry James's theory of fiction.

In writing about the governess's task in *The Turn of the Screw*, James was also constructing a metaphor for his own sense of the contradictions, tensions, and difficulties facing the artist. While influence distorts and limits, it also is necessary to creativity. The governess goes too far in one direction, destroying the work that she seeks to nurture, but James doesn't. Although we may try to affix a definitive interpretation to his story, its success lies in its ability to elude such reductiveness. It maintains a delicacy and balance that make it seem natural in its artistry. Metaphorically speaking, it is as well raised a child as one could wish.

If Henry James found expression for his father's child-rearing method in art, as parents we can turn his art back upon its source to help us raise our children. At the same time, we must know that this is no ordinary method in which the result can be used to measure our success. For to be an artist in the realm of child rearing is to avoid at all costs turning our children into artifacts; it is to avoid superimposing a vision that we hope to realize through them—this was the governess's error. Instead, the artistry of child rearing may only be perceptible in what we learn and how we develop in the act of raising our children. Our method, in other words, produces us far more than it produces them.

Anorexic Thinking

*C*LINICALLY speaking, I have never suffered from anorexia nervosa. I never dropped 25 percent of my original weight or experienced a prolonged cessation of my menstrual period or lost a realistic sense of my body image. These are some of the more easily identifiable symptoms of anorexia, according to the medical literature. And yet, when I was twenty-two, during a particularly unfocused period after graduating from college, when I was "finding myself" in Europe, I became quite obsessively concerned with losing weight.

It was toward the end of my stay in an economically depressed and perpetually rainy city in northern France. I had gone to France as part of a one-year teaching exchange program and was assigned to a secondary school in a city so close to the Belgium border that Parisians shook their heads sadly when they heard it mentioned. The school year had gone well enough, for I had been befriended by a group of French student teachers, most of them from the south, who had been sent north to do their internships and were determined to combat the gloom that the region tended to encourage. But they had left for Paris by the beginning of the summer, while I had stayed on. I was living on the outskirts of town in a shabby pension and each day walking two miles into the city, where I had been engaged as an English tutor to a group of sixteen-year-old girls who were preparing for their "Bac." I was convinced that these girls, who giggled and whispered continuously throughout my lessons, were getting amusement by making fun of certain imperfect parts of my anatomy. I was probably right—French girls are exacting judges of female appearance (they are especially hard on foreigners and, especially, Americans, whom all French seem to feel it a point of national honor to scorn).

As the summer wore on, isolated by both the language and the situation, I came to spend more and more time in developing a stoical self-improvement plan. This consisted of thinking about the food I would not eat and scrupulously choosing and preparing the little food I permitted myself. Such activity was especially challenging in France, where every commercial street is crowded with specialty food stores and where meals are long, ceremonial occasions in which the food itself is handled and talked about with great attention and reverence. At the same time, of course, France is the country most devoted to the cultivation of physical beauty. It worships the female silhouette: the slim figure in the knitted suit, the scarf draped over the neat bosom, the high heel on the well-turned ankle (*taille* is the French word both for the female form and for garment size). The environment was therefore the perfect one to trigger a tendency latent in me both to obsess about food and to deny myself its consumption: the systole and diastole of anorexic thinking. For three months I existed on a meager daily ration: coffee, a small baguette, a slice of cured ham or turkey breast, and one, carefully selected pastry, consumed each evening with an exquisite slowness and meticulousness.

A few more months of that life, and who knows? I might have fallen over the edge into the abyss of delusion and obsession. I might have entered the realm of the clinical anorexic, who, with proud persistence, starves herself to death. Instead, the swirl of activity that greeted me when I returned to the States deflected and diluted that drive. It lost itself in a clutter of small obsessions and excesses. I began to eat meals again. I regained the weight I had lost. And yet the experience gave me an acute understanding of the dynamics of the illness of anorexia nervosa and a fascination with it that persists to this day. Those few months made it possible for me to recognize the shards of anorexic thinking that scattered my history long before I went to France and to see how variations of that thinking endure and are woven into the routine of my daily life. I do not think I am unique in this.

When I begin a discussion of anorexia with my students, I notice that the girls sit at the edge of their seats, mesmerized, gulping down my description with a ghoulish relish. I might be recounting some illicit tale of sexual adventure or some juicy romantic plot. My students and I, despite a generation's difference in age, are linked in some strange way to the lineaments of this illness.

The fascination that anorexia exerts on women suggests to me that we all, to some extent or in some way, suffer from the illness. If we look at certain findings on the disease that recent work has turned up, we may begin to understand why this is. Thirty years ago anorexics were treated in a vacuum as psychologically aberrant individuals, but now experts feel there is a link between a particular kind of family structure and behavior and the emergence of the disease in one family member—generally the daughter. What, according to clinical studies, does such a family, that of a typical anorexic, look like? It is a nuclear family; rarely is there divorce or obvious discord between the parents. It is middle or upper-middle class, well educated and comfortable. Finally, it is a family in which a high premium has been put on achievement and correct behavior. The identified patient tends to be a girl, psychologists say, because girls are especially sensitive to norms, especially eager to please and meet the expectations of their parents.

If one peruses the literature on the illness one begins to see that what is being described is a young girl's wish-fulfillment for herself and her family. The anorexic family is intact, its parental sex roles are generally defined stereotypically, and the anorexic herself is, until the onset of the disease, a "perfect" daughter: an A student who likes to keep her room neat, dress herself carefully and with taste, go shopping with her mother, and sit on her father's lap as he reads the evening paper. What woman does not in some way know this family as an ideal from childhood fairy tales and from sentimental novels, movies, and television?

In seeking a culprit for anorexia nervosa, the tendency has been to hold the pressures of society responsible: to indict advertising and popular entertainment for promoting an unrealistic female aesthetic to girls when they are most vulnerable and impressionable. But, once one begins to understand the generic quality of the family of so many anorexics, the cult of slimness that our society encourages seems to me to recede in importance, to become only a symptom of a more profound cultural complicity. At the root of the illness must be the whole notion of what a family is about and the role in it that the daughter is supposed to play. The "anorexia syndrome" must be inherent in the very idea of the nuclear family—of that little nest of domesticity that crystallized as an institution during the early period of industrialization in Western culture.

It seems as though each time over the past century and a half that the family has threatened to grow slack, to find some other form for itself, or discard its form altogether, another spate of female illnesses has surged into public view and that an anorexic component has always been present in them. At the end of the nineteenth century, Freud brought attention to hysteria. His patients were mostly women with nervous coughs or mysteriously paralyzed arms or legs, but many of them had trouble with food, too. Formal clinical identification of anorexia nervosa was, in fact, made during the nineteenth-century, only the illness wasn't singled out diagnostically very often. There were too many illnesses to contend with that had anorexia-like symptoms—TB, most notably. Yet, if one reads about the lives of nineteenth-century women with attention, one finds physical and psychological clues to the existence of anorexia nervosa in one woman after another, and the effect is especially striking in the cases of literary women. We find Elizabeth Barrett, for example, weighing 87 pounds when she left her father's house to marry Robert Browning; and Henry James's sister, Alice, an invalid dating from her teens, writing regularly in her diary about her digestion; and Emily Brontë refusing to eat in her last illness and exhibiting a stubborn, martyrlike resistance to all medical help.

I am most intrigued, however, by the case of Christina Rossetti, the poet and sister to the Pre-Raphaelite painter Dante Gabriel Rossetti. Rossetti is said to have undergone a radical personality change in early adolescence, when, according to her brother, "her constitution became obviously delicate," and she became introverted, exaggeratedly religious, and obsessively scrupulous in ordering her life. But most suggestive are her poems and particularly her most famous poem, "Goblin Market," written in 1861 when she was twenty-nine and living in relative seclusion with her mother. The poem demonstrates that Rossetti was susceptible to anorexic thinking: it exhibits a pattern that strikingly conforms to the dynamic behind the illness.

The poem begins by describing, in a childish singsong, the cocoon-like existence of two perfect sisters, Lizzie and Laura:

> Golden head by golden head,
> Like two pigeons in one nest
> Folded in each other's wings,
> ....
> Cheek by cheek and breast by breast
> Locked together in one nest.

But the poem proceeds to tell of the sisters' separation and trauma. Laura is one day lured away from her home into the perilous, mossy glen nearby. Here the vile goblin men peddle their wares—an assortment of enticing fruit—to passersby. Laura buys fruit from the goblins and eats, in a gluttonous scene of self-indulgence. She is immediately overwhelmed with a desire for more, but now she can no longer hear the calls of the goblin men, and, deprived of the fruit she craves, she grows "thin and gray." Hoping to save her sister, Lizzie decides to approach the goblin men herself and purchase the fruit to bring back to Laura. There follows a terrible ordeal in which the goblins try to force the fruit on Lizzie but without success:

> Lizzie uttered not a word;
> Would not open lip from lip
> Lest they should cram a mouthful in . . .

Triumphantly resistant, Lizzie finally returns to her sister, who now sucks the juices that still cling to her face and body and, after a terrible paroxysm of vomiting, is cured: restored to her original "golden" state. The poem has been understood to mean many things, but, if one knows about anorexia, one must return to see the fruit as what it is—food— and to recognize the poem's story as an anorexic fantasy. For it proclaims uncritically the dynamic behind the disease: Laura's obsessive desire to eat is countered by Lizzie's greater, saving desire to abstain from eating. In the context of the poem Lizzie's refusal is heroic. It reclaims lost beauty and security. It recaptures a feminine Eden.

In their massive study of nineteenth-century women's writing Sandra M. Gilbert and Susan Gubar noted the prevalence of anorexia, along with hysteria, agoraphobia, and the catchall, neurasthenia, among women in nineteenth-century culture. Anorexia, they argued, was an illness that "carried patriarchal definitions of 'femininity' to absurd extremes": the illness, they said, was a literal and figurative expression of women's deprivation and hunger, of the creative as well as the physical limitations imposed on them by a sexist society. After all, there was Christina Rossetti, cooped up at home with her mother while her brothers cavorted in the Pre-Raphaelite Brotherhood; there was Jane Austen, at home with her sister, Cassandra, doing her writing undercover of the drawing room blotter; there was Elizabeth Barrett, up in her bedroom, an invalid in thrall to a tyrannical father; there was even George Eliot, who, despite taking her life into her own hands and living unmarried with the man of her choice, still suffered the pain of social ostracism so keenly that, when she got the opportunity at the age of sixty, married and signed herself as "Mrs. John Cross." How sad to review the prisonhouse in which women, even the greatest of them, have been confined. Certainly, one can see, as Gilbert and Gubar do, how an illness such as anorexia nervosa might be the logical by-product of this history of female deprivation and imprisonment.

Yet there is also something that this perspective on the illness leaves out. For what about the personal satisfaction that feeds on deprivation, that turns self-denial to creative use, that, lacking all other materials, turns to the body as the only vehicle for expression? Anorexia fascinates many women, I would suggest, because we know that the illness is not just a pathology bred by patriarchal culture that we must brutally cut away. It is also entwined with something basic to our identity.

Let me explain. Anorexia takes to a fatal extreme the impulse to view oneself artistically—and I claim this as a feminine impulse. It is the impulse that I feel when I enter a department store and see the counters of makeup, all promising to improve the face I present to the world. Coppery eyeshadow or pressed translucent powder with little gold specks or chinaberry gloss for the lips—these appeal to me as potential enhancements for the canvas that is myself, a canvas that also calls out to be continually restored: the hair frizzes in rainy weather, the face gets blotchy around the chin, crow's-feet form under the eyes. For the anorexic this drive to enhance is also the ultimate attempt at restoration—an attempt to restore the smooth and fragile child of preadolescence. At the same time, it is a reaching for something new. For the drive to get thin eventually disconnects itself from a sense of the thing being acted upon—the body—and becomes purely an idea to which the body is made to minister. One could argue that the anorexic is a true Platonist in that she works to make the body into the idea, to make it, in effect, disappear into the idea.

A great deal has been written about the superficiality of a culture that focuses on the beautification of the female body as much as ours does, but I think a reverse argument can be made: that female body consciousness is the extreme of creative expression. It is the using of oneself as both the source and the end of creative expression. There is a dazzling efficiency and self-sufficiency about this concern for appearance once you start to think about it. And the anorexic takes this self-sufficiency a step further, for she fashions her idea out of nothing. If I need cosmetics to improve myself, the anorexic does better and needs not to need, does without, subtracts rather than adds. Like the artist working with negative space, she works not with what is there but with what is not. In this she is more than a hunger artist; she is a body artist akin to the bodybuilder, though with a goal that is not muscled definition and bulk but frailty and delicacy. The anorexic's will power is directed toward the physical goal of making her body thin as air, of *re*making herself in the service of an aesthetic that seems to be entirely her own.

Or perhaps one can take this further still and argue that the anorexic's drive is an overreaching of the artistic impulse. The sense of power that anorexics experience is a form of megalomania. It comes from a feeling of having usurped the role of divinity, of being one's own maker. The anorexic defies her parents not only by refusing to listen to them anymore but also by symbolically rejecting their legacy of life and substituting her own death-driven agenda. In this context the role of the mirror acquires particular significance. I am reminded of the psychoanalytic theory of Jacques Lacan that points to the "mirror stage" of development. This is the point at which the child sees herself for the first time in the gaze of her mother and enters into an "imaginary" realm that will be solidified and padlocked through the acquisition of language. For the anorexic the mirror becomes a symbol that exhibits that socially acquired self to her and then, in the shrinking image that the mirror reflects as she continues to diet, begins to record what seems like an escape from that imprisoning false self.

A work of literature that records this mirror effect with uncanny power is Charlotte Brontë's *Jane Eyre*. Early in the novel Jane is punished by her unsympathetic guardian by being confined for the night in an unused room of the house. The room is red, with all that this suggests of female adolescent initiation. The room also happens to be the one in which the master of the house had died. In the course of her confinement Jane passes in front of a large looking glass and catches a glimpse of herself and her surroundings reflected back at her:

> All looked colder and darker in that visionary hollow than in reality: and the strange little figure there gazing at me, with a white face and arms specking the gloom, and glittering eyes of fear moving where all else was still, had the effect of a real spirit: I thought it like one of the tiny phantoms, half fairy, half imp, Bessie's evening stories represented as coming up out of lone, ferny dells in moors, and appearing before the eyes of belated travellers.

The mirror, in turning back an image of the heroine that is pale and spiritlike, works strangely to empower her. She idealizes her own etherealness and asserts her resemblance to magical creatures: fairies and imps. It is as though the ghost of the room's former master has been transmuted, femininized, into herself, as though she is now in the position to turn on that masculine ghost, being more ghostly than he, and to become an antidote as well to the massive furniture and dark surfaces in the room that confines her. When, a few paragraphs later, she feels a rush of injustice toward her oppressors and contemplates how she may achieve escape, she hits on the expedient of "never eating or drinking more, and letting myself die." Jane does not literally starve herself, but the novel does chart a course of resistance involving self-effacement and self-denial through which she ultimately triumphs as the heroine Brontë has determined she should be. The mirror, one could argue, has early in the novel shown her an idea of herself as a spirit—a ghostly, glittering, white-faced little creature—and this idea of herself will sustain her against the dark, fleshy oppressiveness of the other characters.

Clearly, Charlotte Brontë was susceptible to the allure of anorexic thinking, and I am, too, for I have gone on too long about the creative and heroic associations attached to the disease. I don't want to be accused of putting anorexics on a pedestal, of elevating them as martyrs to some perverse ideal of femininity. If I do this, I have sunk myself so deep into anorexic thinking as to have ceased to be a responsible critic any longer. For there is a difference between metaphorical anorexia, which I think is the creative drive behind much women's writing, and anorexic behavior, the reality of self-starvation. While the writer can change her world to her specifications, the anorexic cannot and hence works relentlessly on changing herself. The mirror image continually frustrates her: instead of being freed to see herself made over through her own efforts, made thin at last, she continues to see herself as fat, even when she is only skin and bones, until, finally, she is dead. This seems to reflect the profound fallacy that lies at the root of anorexia. For the self-representation the anorexic strives for in trying to become thin is based on a social ideal; it is, therefore, mired in the very constraints that she wishes to escape. In other words, the anorexic's desire to escape her body produces a double bind: the more she tries to achieve an authentic self-representation, the more she becomes enmeshed in a web of social expectations and preconceptions that puts her goal out of reach.

This may help us to explain why anorexia appeared to become epidemic in the 1960s, precisely the time when the first wave of the contemporary feminist movement was breaking on the consciousness of society. It was as though the illness arrived as a counterforce to feminist thinking, a means by which women physically registered the conditioning of centuries that their intellectual selves were seeking to reject. Anorexic behavior, in this context, emerges as a policing mechanism by which women are forced back into traditional roles even as they strive to be free of these roles.

Yet I can't help returning to my earlier observation that anorexia speaks to women in a powerful, if macabre, voice. It speaks of a history that cannot be obliterated and is the basis for a distinctively feminine aesthetic. Keeping anorexic thinking apart from anorexic behavior is a challenge. I suspect it is *the* challenge at the heart of postmodern feminism. But perhaps an aesthetic can only become powerful when it contains an element of danger—when it risks breaking out of its artificial constraints and spilling over into life. Many female writers seem to be balancing on the tightrope to which I am referring. Sylvia Plath in "Lady Lazarus" writes of dying as an art and boasts of her ability to resurrect herself for an appreciative audience:

It's the theatrical

Comeback in broad day
To the same place, the same face, the same brute
Amused shout:

"A miracle!"

More than just the physical recovery from a bungled suicide, the "theatrical comeback" to which she refers is the poetry she continues to
write. And it seems no coincidence that her greatest poems were written just before she succeeded, finally, in killing herself. I see Plath's
death as a final pushing beyond to what the poems have been all the
while substituting for and, in this sense, holding off.

Louise Glück, whose poem "Dedication to Hunger" is explicitly
about suffering from anorexia, also makes the equation between art
and the death drive:

... I remember
lying in bed at night
touching the soft, digressive breasts,
touching, at fifteen,
the interfering flesh
that I would sacrifice
until the limbs were free
of blossom and subterfuge: I felt
what I feel now, aligning these words—
it is the same need to perfect,
of which death is the mere byproduct.

Glück's poem is permeated with the sense that, by choosing to write
and not to starve herself to death, she has triumphed over a great
adversary but also that she has settled for an aesthetic compromise: life
cannot encompass art as completely as death can. Emily Dickinson,
more than a century earlier, had, in her cryptic fashion, implied the
same thing:

Me from Myself—to banish—
Had I Art—
Impregnable my Fortress
Unto All Heart—

But since Myself—assault Me—
How have I peace
Except by subjugating
Consciousness?

For all that Dickinson's poem is a struggle to effect the feat of self-ban-
ishment, it can only point beyond itself, beyond consciousness. The
poet has not "art" enough to annihilate herself. Although it seems that
Dickinson's drive was to twist language to allow her to slip through it
and escape into air, her poems announce that she existed—a solid, living body—to write them.

The goal, it would seem, is to keep a leash on art. This can be difficult
and tiring. It requires a good sense of balance to maintain the line that
separates aesthetics from experience: writing books and painting pic-
tures, decorating apartments and buying clothes, putting on makeup
and going on diets. Where does the line get crossed? At what point
does the objectively artful become the self-destructively self-improving? I've drawn the line at different places at different times in my life,
and my present awareness is no guarantee against some future loss of
balance. I do know that my own body stands behind all these choices as
the ultimate canvas, the place where self-expression can be most dis-
tilled and personalized. If this self-referencing aesthetic is part of my
legacy as a woman, I can only hope to continue to spare the real body
and find the metaphorical one upon which to do creative work.

The Good Class

*I*T is the fifth week of the course, nearing midterm, and the class sits sullenly waiting for the hour to end. I feel the resentment in the long, inert silence that greets my questions. "What do you think of the opening paragraph?" I ask with aggressive cheerfulness. "Any thoughts? Any suggestions for improvement?" I have been a teacher for over fifteen years, and yet the thing I hate most is sounding like a teacher. It means that whatever I'm doing isn't working, that my voice is echoing in a void.

The students in this particular class, Writing for Business, Section 5, Tues Th, 10–11:30, have, from the beginning, been resentful and unaccommodating, but today their discontent seems to weigh more heavily. I have just returned an assignment—a "memo" aimed at an imaginary supervisor regarding a shortfall in the budget of an imaginary company—and they are not happy with the grade I have penciled, as unobtrusively as possible, in the corner of the page. I almost never give below a C, but even a B makes these students furious. Who am I to give them a B when their father's friend, a top insurance adjuster, looked the thing over and said it was fine? At such times, I confess, teaching absolutely depresses me. Partially, this is because I hate having to explain the value of correct writing to students who are not about to be convinced; partially, because I think maybe they're right—that their father's friend does know better what counts and what doesn't when it comes to a business memo.

Writing for Business is relatively new to the undergraduate university curriculum. Over the period of its short life, however, it has moved from being a peripheral, low-prestige course to being the bread and butter of many English departments. As a result, in schools like mine that pride themselves on their practical orientation, there are now very few literature professors who can avoid teaching if not it then something like it: Technical Writing, Professional Editing, Corporate Communication, Writing for the Media—the permutations on the professional writing concept are endless. While such courses were not

57

exactly conceived to replace the specialized literature courses that once constituted the university English curriculum, they effectively have done so. For, as the literature offerings shrink, the service courses expand, and the teachers originally hired to teach the one are shuttled over to teach the other. Thus, I find myself teaching more sections of Writing for Business and fewer courses on The Novel, Nineteenth-Century Nonfiction Prose, and Romantic Poetry. Obviously, this shift requires that I master a new body of material, but the problem for me lies less in the subject matter than in the way the subject matter changes the shape and style of the classroom experience as I value it.

If, over lunch, a teacher of literature happens to say that he or she had a "good class" that day, we in the profession all know what this means. A good class makes teaching worthwhile, not in the sense that one feels one has imparted knowledge or brought students closer to some intellectual ideal, though this may very well be the by-product and the justification given. A good class really has to do with a feeling of excitement that those involved take away from it. Students lose something when such classes cease being taught because they don't get to experience a certain kind of intellectual and emotional intensity. Education, transpiring without this intensity, breeds resentment—a hunger for engagement with ideas and feelings that students and, arguably, teachers too have no other means of satisfying.

To comprehend the value of a good class one really has to experience one, but, as it seems likely that more and more people will graduate from college without ever having done so, let me attempt to describe a recent example—a class that occurred in a modestly enrolled poetry survey that I get to teach occasionally. The course is a kind of stray in the curriculum, otherwise known as a "free elective," which means that it doesn't fulfill any requirement for any particular major but simply adds to the general number of credits that a student needs for graduation. Such courses are consistently under-enrolled at the university where I teach and are often canceled when enrollment falls below the minimum requirement of twelve students. This course had squeaked through with twelve (though one student had dropped during the first week) and so had survived the administrative ax by one (alleged) body. It was the fifth week of the term, and I had assigned the class a selection of poems from Blake's *Songs of Innocence and of Experi-*

ence. We were to begin that day with the first poem in the collection, the one titled simply "Introduction."

Let me pause here to explain that the class in question was in no way out of the ordinary. None of the students was a literary prodigy, few were even humanities majors. What I had was a group of juniors and seniors fairly representative of the first-generation college students attending the urban university where I teach. What distinguished this group from my Writing for Business students was that they were not angry. They saw no cause to harden themselves against me or against Blake. That's all it takes, really: a class not predisposed against you, and a good poem, one that's friendly to visitors. Had the class been Writing for Business, the chairs would have been filled, but the atmosphere would have been leaden. They would have resented me for keeping them from the April day outside. But Blake's poem had something of the bright crispness of the day. It carried itself lightly but with the seductiveness that comes with not seeming to try too hard:

> Piping down the valleys wild
> Piping songs of pleasant glee
> On a cloud I saw a child,
> And he laughing said to me,
>
> "Pipe a song about a Lamb,"
> So I piped with merry chear;
> "Piper pipe that song again"—
> So I piped, he wept to hear.
>
> "Drop thy pipe thy happy pipe
> Sing thy songs of happy chear";
> So I sung the same again
> While he wept with joy to hear.

Those are the first three stanzas of the poem (it has only five), and the three boys in the front row quickly set things in motion as they might a soccer ball on an open field. Contrary to popular belief, a class does not follow the strongest, the most vocal, or the most intelligent students; it follows those who exude something more ineffable, call it charm or glamour. These boys, their long legs and large sneakered feet stretched out lazily in front of them, had, like the poem, an effortlessness about them that was glamorous. They seemed free not only of social constraint but of history itself, to belong only to one another and to the immediacy of the class.

"It's strange that the child orders the piper to play, not the other way around," comments one of the boys, gulping from a can of Coke. "The Pied Piper in that story led the children, but here it's the child who leads the piper."

"But the child is on a cloud, special, like an angel, not an ordinary child," explains the boy in the baseball cap next to him.

"Maybe the child is only imaginary, a fantasy of the piper's," returns the first. "Or part of his imagination—the way you say someone creative has the imagination of a child."

"Or maybe the poet has this real child," begins the third boy, who's drive is always for literal solutions, "and this flesh-and-blood child reminds him of himself as a child [he pauses to get the logic right and tie everything up]. This makes him think about the kinds of things that children would like to hear."

"Which would make the poet the piper," adds the first boy, an observation that initiates a temporary break in the discussion. The boys have done their part; they've kicked the poem into the class. There is a sense of expectation now, of ideas waiting to be generated. We are approaching another level of engagement with the poem, and the class catches its breath before it takes hold again. I should add here that a good class is, like a good poem, plastic, expansive. As it proceeds, it seems to become more indistinct yet more like itself, to lose individual outlines yet gain distinguishing characteristics. Thus, the loose-limbed ease of the three boys in the front row seemed to bring into relief the lush black lashes shadowing the eyes of the girl near the door and the sweet smile of the shy boy in the back; to make interesting the slight stammer breaking the breathless speech patterns of the girl who always hurries in late, held over by her biology lab, and to highlight the exotic precision with which the Vietnamese student, dressed with Sunday School neatness, delivers his slowly worded responses.

"Why," asks the Vietnamese student now, "does the child weep? How does this weeping relate to the repeating of the song and to the child so lately laughing?"

"To repeat is to lose something," says the girl with the black lashes solemnly.

"Mass produced, mechanical, not authentic," the Vietnamese student offers.

"Does the poem support this idea further?" I ask, not wanting to press, the rhythm of response being fragile. The class shifts its gaze to the last two stanzas:

"Piper sit thee down and write
In a book that all may read"—
So he vanish'd from my sight.
And I pluck'd a hollow reed,

And I made a rural pen,
And I stain'd the water clear,
And I wrote my happy songs
Every child may joy to hear.

"'And, and, and'—the staining that is writing," offers the shy student, "technology, mass production, pollution—."

"The poem gets more mechanical as it talks about the repetition that comes with making the piper's songs available to a large a-audience," adds the hurried student with the stammer.

"But also gaining in communication, spreading joy," counters the girl with the lashes.

"The poet has only the assumption he'll spread joy or only the hope," explains the Vietnamese student. "'Every child *may* joy to hear.' The child who first inspired, the one on the cloud—*he* has vanished."

"He's lost the inspiration, the child in himself; he's become a hack," announces the boy with the Coke.

"It's also questioning the typical belief that technological progress makes things better," adds the shy student.

"Or that poems are worth the hassle of studying them," announces the most disengaged student in the class, who rarely speaks. "The poet was better in the beginning, before he became a poet, when he didn't answer to anyone, just piped what he wanted," he announces in a sarcastic tone.

The class, it seems to me at this point, has not just interpreted; it has repeated the poem, demonstrating, both in the responses given and in the way each individual produced these responses, the innocence that experience crushes, the experience that simulates or recuperates innocence, the trade-off between modes of being and kinds of understanding, the inevitable movement from some possibly illusory origin, some silence or random state or solitude, into what?—this discussion, this here and now of interpretation and debate.

"The poem," says the disengaged student, now engaged and turning his attention to the class, "was better when it was simple, before we got our hands on it."

"But that's gone," says the girl with the beautiful lashes, "and here we are with it. There's no going back." (To me it is clear that she likes the unengaged student and wants very much for him to notice her.)

"Well, it's not my choice we're here. I'd rather be back where I started." Though he is talking about the poem, he seems to have left it for something else—his dissatisfaction with his life, perhaps his failure to please his parents. "It's only been downhill for me since kindergarten," he finishes angrily, letting the hostility, that bottled-up hostility of my Writing for Business students, spill over, get expressed in words, to be received by this challenging yet sympathetic audience of the class.

"That's because you don't look around you and see what's there—," flares the girl, a reply so bald the class seems shaken by it, especially since he finally looks at her and keeps quiet.

Such things do tend to happen at the end of discussions of poems, when the poem opens into life, when the ecstasy of merging into the class mind has dissipated and the class gets back to being individuals again, only now connected to one another in a new way.

The intense feeling generated in a good class cannot be prolonged beyond its time or replicated at will or even talked about later with any clarity or persuasiveness—though, admittedly, I am trying to do that here (and will probably be accused of banality and naive enthusiasm by some readers for doing so). The awkwardness and embarrassment that come with talking about a good class resemble the awkwardness and embarrassment that come with talking about religious experience. I don't find this surprising. Teaching literature in a university carries with it something of what once was associated with religious calling. Like religious experience, it involves ecstatic moments—fleeting, but intense and potentially transformative. Like religion, it also teaches an approach to life. For the debate that happens around a work of literature is about the valuing and exploration of ambiguity and overdetermination, about learning to express difference and to incorporate difference. It is also about learning to express joy, anger, and appreciation in an authentic way within the restraining bounds of a classroom—about how to turn intellect to feeling and feeling to intellect, and about how to return to the pragmatics of life when the class is over.

An overdetermined business memo, one that says more than one thing, that is subtle and ambiguous, is, generally speaking, a bad memo. Business writing belongs to the world of practice in which one strives not for open-endedness but for closure: for getting the job done. For this reason it seems to me that an imaginary business memo, the kind I ask my students to write for a grade, is an absurdity. The memo should be learned in apprenticeship, scribbled over by a real, not an imaginary, supervisor, made better by trial and error. Severed from an instrumental context, it becomes perverse, a symbol of the bankruptcy of ideas and of the failure of the concept of higher education.

But a poem belongs perhaps most of all *in* a classroom. After all, there is a *fit* between the form of a class and the form of a poem. I am always struck by the way the facets of a good poem break up in a classroom into voices and how these voices, the expression of individuals shaped by distinct backgrounds and experiences, are able to make available the full meaning of the poem as I imagine its author would have wanted. That author is, of course, an imaginary being, brought to life through the discussion. But I can't think of a greater tribute to a "real" author than of being imagined by a good class.

I also see poetry as a vehicle through which the university can do what it is supposed to do at its best. John Henry Newman in *The Idea of University* drew a distinction between education and instruction: we are instructed, he explained, "in manual exercises, in the fine and useful arts, in trades, and in ways of business. . . . But education is a higher word; it implies an action upon our mental nature, and the formation of a character; it is something individual and permanent, and is commonly spoken of in connexion with religion and virtue." The university, he concludes, is a place of education. The distinction Newman draws may seem artificial and high-flown to our present sensibility, and it may be impractical to expect students to defer instruction toward a career. But I find Newman's distinction helpful in justifying my belief that poetry belongs in the university—that the discussion of poetry distills the educational process. Without such discussion it seems likely that the individual element in our natures "commonly spoken of in connection with religion and virtue," which Newman already saw threatened a century ago, will wither, to the eternal loss of students and educators and of that wider arena in which our humanness gets tested in more mundane activity.

Speech and Silence

*A*S a girl, I was always a lively and fluent speaker in the privacy of
my family. But this was purely a matter of what I call domestic
talk: gossip, emotional expression, descriptive narration. In the other,
the public arena of the classroom, I was one of the perennially silent—
a good student who took notes but never raised her hand. Public
speech seemed to involve monumental effort. It meant coming up with
something logical to say, finding the right words in which to say it, con-
trolling the timbre and volume of my voice as I said it, and (most
daunting of all) being prepared to rebut anyone who disagreed with
me. When I did manage to speak, it was with the point I had to make
carefully suspended in my head the way one hangs on to a telephone
number in walking from one room to another. The result was hurried
and cryptic: a painful fracturing of the silence to which I wanted as
quickly as possible to return.

Recent work in gender-linked cognition has studied the behavior
of girls faced with expressing themselves in different contexts. In the
classroom or in public forums, researchers say, girls tend to efface
themselves and leave it to boys to provide an original answer or to challenge the teacher. On the other hand, as my own case shows, the stereotype involving speech and silence undergoes a reversal when one
moves from the public to the private sphere. Women from an early age
express themselves at home with greater ease and elaboration than
men do. The dynamic has been made familiar to us from TV sitcoms
and from the marital profiles featured on "Oprah Winfrey" and "Dona-
hue": an emotionally expressive wife and a taciturn husband—she
nags, he withdraws; she wants more talk, he less.

Gender-stereotyped behavior such as this raises some interesting
questions not only about the relationship of the sexes but also about the
relationship between speech and silence itself. Is speech in one sphere
related to silence in another? Do women speak more privately because
they feel silenced publicly, and are men more silent at home because
they must "husband" their resources for public talk—and action?

Such questions assume that there are clear and distinct divisions between public and private, male and female, inside and outside. This is both true and false. Western culture is built on an ideology of such distinctions, and yet the whole thrust of our culture over the course of this century has been toward the dismantling, or at least the revision, of this ideology. This revision is in no way complete, and perhaps it never can be. But what we seem to have at the moment is a simple sexual complementarity shadowing our lives that has been superimposed upon by revised relational patterns—patterns whose existence makes it possible for me to speak on this subject as I am doing here. In short, gender and other societal roles (for, as I shall argue, minorities in our society have a relationship to speech and silence akin to that of women) may appear to conform to an uncomplicated age-old structure, but a closer examination reveals that the structure of these roles and the related nature and value of speech and silence are far more mixed and changeable than they may at first appear to be.

To demonstrate this, let me begin by considering in more detail the simple sexual ideology that continues to cast its shadow over us and that supplies us with much of the vocabulary through which a revised sexual and social ideology is being shaped. We can find the foundation for this ideology articulated in nineteenth-century English novels, the PR department of sexual myth-making for Western culture. As a genre, the English novel concerns itself for the most part with domestic space and with domestic talk. Yet, though it makes this space and this talk central, it does so as a means of reinforcing a divison of power that gives precedence to what lies outside of it: that is, public space and public talk, both of which it associates with men. English novels are, to use one literary critic's phrase, "heroine's texts," but only insofar as they reinforce the rightness of domestic talk for women. Their implicit secondary message is that women are silent in the "real" world outside the domestic sphere (and outside the novel) in which men engage in the talk that counts. Jane Austen's heroines are adept at domestic chitchat and stand at the center of her novels, but it is her men, reticent and peripheral though they are within the space of her narrative, who determine the outcome of the plot. They must propose to the heroines in order for the "proper" conclusion to be achieved.

Austen pokes fun at her heroes along the way, but her mockery only goes so far, or, rather, only takes place within certain specified contexts. Take the scene in which Elizabeth Bennet, the heroine of *Pride and Prejudice*, chides the seemingly arrogant and aloof Darcy (whom she is destined to marry) for not pursuing conversation after he has asked her to dance. "It is *your* turn to say something, Mr. Darcy," Elizabeth finally declares after receiving a monosyllabic response to her last attempt at conversation—"I talked about the dance, and *you* ought to make some kind of remark on the size of the room, or the number of couples." When he then questions the need for such "talk by rule" while dancing, she explains: "One must speak a little, you know. It would look odd to be entirely silent for half an hour together." But the exchange, for all that it gives the heroine and her creator a chance to make fun of the rich and estimable Darcy, is what I would call reinforcing parody: it parodies social stereotypes as a means of reinforcing them. Far from serving to convince women that they should expect their men to come to them well versed in the art of small talk, the scene demonstrates that good women know how to talk and good men don't when they find themselves on the dance floor together for the first time. Although Elizabeth chides Darcy for his initial reticence, it is a reticence that ultimately serves as a mark of his good character, whereas the facile Mr. Wickham, who plys Elizabeth with words at their first meeting, turns out to be a cad.

More extreme examples of how English novelists of the period helped to publicize the rightness of male silence in the domestic sphere come to mind in Charlotte Brontë's Mr. Rochester and her sister Emily's even more taciturn Heathcliff. Both these men are, at least initially, closemouthed in their dealings with the heroines. Yet, in the public sphere outside the novels' domestic space, they presumably exhibit the rhetorical skills needed to run estates, build businesses, and make investments. Heathcliff may run away from Wuthering Heights in a fit of inarticulate jealous rage early in the novel, but he returns a few years later with the manners and dress of a gentleman and having conveniently amassed a fortune. This could not have been achieved in surly silence. Similarly, toward the end of *Pride and Prejudice*, when Lydia disappears with the disreputable Wickham, it is Darcy who, out of sight of the drawing room, comes secretly to the rescue and works things out "in town" (Elizabeth only finds out about his intervention secondhand through her aunt).

Of course, we are made to suspect that something more than talk assists these men outside the novel. Knowing Heathcliff as we do, we imagine that his success must have involved some strong-arm tactics, while Darcy appears to have relied on another kind of pressure—that embodied in the adage "money talks": in order to convince Wickham to marry Lydia, he settles a generous sum on the couple. The implication in both these cases is that talk in the public sphere is connected with something beyond the reach of words, with the power of violence or money (though the details are generally left unspecified as not proper to domestic ears).

The nonverbal, "active" component of public expression that the English novel hints at undergoes significant exaggeration when we turn to the American tradition. While the assumption in the English novel is that the male hero carries on his real life in a world in which public speech is complemented by action, the American hero, most dramatically represented in the form of the cowboy or frontiersman, has action replace speech altogether. That this revision of the English masculine ideal should occur in America is understandable. As a young country, we had no elaborate social structure to maintain and were faced with great vistas of open land. A desire for appropriation would logically supersede a desire for class status.

But the celebration of male action in American culture would also create a crucial imbalance in the sexual ideology inherited from England. By substituting action for speech in the public realm, the American hero succeeded less in denigrating public speech (indeed, the American myth continues to support public speech so long as it is goal oriented) than in vindicating men's silence in the domestic realm in a more all-encompassing way than was possible for their English counterparts. The message that emerges historically in American culture is that silence is not a function of male limitation as it complements female aptitude in this area (albeit limitation looked upon positively, as Jane Austen's novels teach) but, rather, a sign of directness, health, and wholeness. If real life consists of action, then speech becomes a repression—a form of deviousness or, worse, cowardice—and those who don't need to speak are the best and most authentic individuals in the society. From the point of view of gender ideology the most salient by-product of this mythology is not only the way it further denigrates domestic talk (that which women stereotypically do well) but the way it also destroys the implicit reciprocity built into the nineteenth-century English model of male-female relations. Although men were more powerful than women in the English tradition, they were felt to need women to help them function in private life: to provide emotional and rhetorical guidance. Thus, Darcy concedes at the end of *Pride and Prejudice* that Elizabeth taught him the importance of "civility." The American hero, whose silence is the mark of his perfect integration into reality, is self-sufficient. He needs a woman only for certain pragmatic and reproductive services. No wonder that in so many westerns the female lead figures as an encounter peripheral to the plot. Even when marriage and domesticity seem promised at the end of the movie, this is presented as a temporary or superficial addition to the life of the hero, who will presumably continue his mobile existence and his active solitary battle against the forces of evil.

Henry James, a writer perhaps more acutely attuned to shifts in the American scene for having lived most of his adult life abroad, grasped the unique quality of the American masculine ideal in one of his earliest novels. *The American,* first published in 1876, treats the allure and the limitations attached to the American myth of heroic silence. The novel features a laconic protagonist named Christopher Newman, who is ultimately defeated in his bid to marry a French noblewoman by the wily schemes of her family—by their aptitude for devious talk and his inaptitude for such talk. In simple terms they call his bluff. But, although Newman loses the object of his desire, James makes it clear that his refusal to speak about a crime committed by his enemies (though to speak might have gained him what he wants) is the sign of his heroism. At the same time, however, James suggests something more—namely, that Newman, being the self-sufficient hero that he is, doesn't really need the heroine he thinks he wants, and hence he deserves to lose her (though whether she deserves to be buried alive in a convent is another issue). In this context Newman's honorable silence is the silence of being able to do without—of mythic wholeness.

It should be noted that James's novel reveals an essential irony at the center of the American myth. In refusing to speak, Newman refuses to act, pointing up how, in certain contexts at least, speech and action are not opposite but coincident, a fact implicitly grasped in the English tradition, which always assumes that the hero needs to learn domestic speech from the heroine because, without it, he's liable to miss certain important opportunities (as, for example, Darcy almost loses his chance to win Elizabeth with his first uncouth marriage proposal). James even indicates that part of the reason why the noblewoman's family ultimately refuses to accept Newman is because he was unable to make the expected social conversation at a party they had given in his honor. The implication: had he been able to engage in "good" talk to begin with, he might never have been placed in the position of having to engage in the kind of "bad" talk that his sense of honor recoils from. Furthermore, at the bottom of Newman's unwillingness to talk against the people who have wronged him lies a suspicion that he himself harbors of whether he could do so convincingly. Would he, in short, be able to speak the words with proper fluency and authority? Would anyone believe him or care to believe him? The ambivalence that Newman exhibits at the end of the novel, while he watches the incriminating evidence against his enemies burn up in the fireplace where he has thrown it, suggests that he is supposed to be in doubt about what the value and source of his silence really is. Faced with Newman's ambivalence, the reader is encouraged to regard his silence with ambivalence as well.

In his later work James would take up the same theme but with a sterner eye to social effects. He would attribute a basic lack of synchrony between men and women in his society to the kind of masculine values held by Newman. In his late collection of essays, *The American Scene*, written after visiting the United States for what would be the last time, he complains that women are ascendant in America insofar as a kind of aimless domestic talk has engulfed social existence. "American life," he writes, ". . . fall[s] upon the earnest view as a society of women 'located' in a world of men . . . the men supplying, as it were all the canvas, and the women all the embroidery." Men, James seems to be saying, in their blank ("canvas"-like) self-sufficiency, have removed themselves from a dynamic relationship with women, with the result that social interaction has become trivialized (mere "embroidery"). For James sexual reciprocity is a metaphor for the tension and complementarity inherent in communication itself; without it culture grows weak and impoverished.

What does the case of Christopher Newman, of Owen Wister's epically taciturn Virginian, and of the Gary Coopers and John Waynes who succeeded them on screen tell us about the ideological meaning of speech and silence in the United States? The American landscape of the frontier and the promiscuousness of democracy itself seem to have produced in those who were given greatest access to it—that is, white males—a myth of self-sufficiency that found justification in heroic action. Yet, taken to its logical extreme, this myth becomes an image of satiation and stasis: the man who doesn't need to speak also doesn't need home, family, or human relationship of any kind. The hero becomes a heroic icon. Culturally speaking, something as inert as an icon can only hold us for so long. The eye wanders to the background, and it is to this background that we have, for the past forty years, begun to attend.

In the landscape behind the hero are the "Indians"—all those whose silence is not voluntary and replete with meaning but, instead, enforced and expendable. When we shift the lens and focus on the background character, the outsider to the American myth, we find an individual whose personal drama is different from that of the hero but no less compelling. Far from being self-sufficient or satiated, the outsider is needy, hungry, acutely aware of not having and, most importantly from the point of view of self-identity, of not being heard. Thus, unsurprisingly, when we are dealing with the outsiders to American culture, whether women or other minorities, they are defined by talk—not argumentation, mind you, that speech of the public sphere that supposes a rational goal or an end in action—but some version of private talk that works both to reveal the speaker in all his or her cultural and personal uniqueness and to integrate him or her into the fabric of the society, the custom of the country.

Take the case of first-generation Jews in American society after World War II. A background sketch for the particular relationship of this group to speech (and writing) can be found in an early short story by Cynthia Ozick entitled "Envy; or, Yiddish in America." The story concerns itself with a Yiddish poet, one Hershel Edelshtein, desperate to be read and appreciated but fated to oblivion, or so he believes, because of his reliance on a dead language. Tortured by frustrated ambition, he recites a continuous litany of his discontents in his broken English: writing letters to publishers, needling old friends, and, in a climactic scene, harassing a young woman, a first-generation American who happens to be fluent in Yiddish, trying to persuade her to serve as his translator. Edelshtein is both a metaphor for the drive that fuels the American Jewish writer and the progenitor of that writer. Still yoked to Yiddish for his creative expression, since he is too old to master English fluently, he is blocked from being heard, though he continues to berate the world around him for its refusal to hear. The kind of "private" whining, complaining talk that Ozick ascribes to her character is precisely what in first-generation Jewish writers (of which Ozick herself is one) becomes a hallmark of their artistic expression. The verbal tics of their fathers and mothers, developed out of the frustration of feeling themselves silenced in the public sphere, become the expression they adopt for their art. Saul Bellow's novel *Herzog* and Alfred Kazin's memoir *Walker in the City* both publicize and celebrate a private, frustrated Jewish speech. Perhaps the best example can be found in Philip Roth's early novel, *Portnoy's Complaint*. As is well-known (and as Roth has never allowed us to forget), when this book first appeared it scandalized the Jewish community, while it also catapulted its author to fame. It was an extraordinary feat of expressiveness that both associated itself with an outsider group and acted as an initiatory strategy. In its exaggerated ethnic quality, its pointed cultural and self-revelations, it pushed its way into the consciousness of a public readership and, in a sweep, opened up what would thereafter be considered an acceptable subject matter and style for good fiction.

Something similar can be said to have happened more recently with African-American women's fiction. Black writers, critics say, had traditionally felt compelled to write for propogandistic purposes, to assume, even during the Black Arts movement of the 1960s, when so much important black poetry and fiction were being generated, a public voice directed at an implicitly white audience. Female African-American writers today, though heir to the race consciousness of that movement, have shrugged off these public constraints and embraced private speech: talk among themselves and for themselves. Thus, Gloria Naylor begins *Mama Day* with two run-on sentences:

> You were picking your teeth with a plastic straw—I know, I know, it wasn't really a straw, it was a coffee stirrer. But, George, let's be fair, there are two little openings in those things that you could possibly suck liquid through if you were desperate enough, so I

think I'm justified in calling it a straw since dumps like that Third Avenue coffee shop had no shame in calling it a coffee stirrer, when the stuff they poured into your cup certainly didn't qualify as coffee.

What bravado lurks in this aggressively private entry into narrative. Toni Morrison begins her early novel *The Bluest Eye* with a comparable breaking away from public speech. She frames her story with the primer story "Dick and Jane"—clipped and minimalistic white bread prose ("Here is the house. It is green and white. It has a red door.")— then follows with her own outsider rendering: an unpunctuated repetition accelerated until it becomes a blur of letters on the page. This is her prelude to the story of Pecola, the girl who has existed outside the margins of all past stories, just as she has stood outside the margins of conventional, proper, white-defined society. At the end of Morrison's *Sula* Nel, reunited with her childhood friend and recalling their past together, dissolves into speech: "'Oh Lord, Sula,' she cried, 'girl girl girlgirlgirl.'" Overladen with emotion and with history, these words seem to be about filling up a void that has been empty too long; there isn't time to be correct or orderly. Nel cares only about finally connecting, verbally, with her friend.

All of Alice Walker's novels and stories are experiments in the use of the private voice, but *The Color Purple* is perhaps her most dramatic demonstration. It is composed as a series of letters from the protagonist Celie, a poor black Southern woman, written first to God then to her sister Nettie in Africa. If you knew the plot but didn't read the book, it might sound like a work of propaganda—a chronicle of the injustices and abuses perpetrated against Celie and of Celie's resilience in the face of them. But the voice of the letters makes such a label seem false. Walker's novel is as much about the wonder of breaking silence, about Celie's promiscuous love of words, as it is a story about pain, loss, hope, and salvation. Here is an early conversation between Celie and Shug, the woman who will become Celie's lover and friend, and it captures the way the relationship will be grounded in a rich, funny, domestic exchange of words:

I ast Shug Avery what she want for breakfast. She say, what yall got? I say ham, grits, eggs, biscuits, coffee, sweet milk or butter milk, flapjacks. Jelly and jam.

She say, Is that all? What about orange juice, grapefruit, straw-
berries and cream. Tea. Then she laugh.

I don't want none of your damn food, she say. Just gimme a cup
of coffee and hand me my cigarettes.

African-American women's fiction sometimes feels like its mow-
ing you down with words; it has all the force of generations of repression behind it. In this respect it resembles (though many may balk at
the comparison) the African-American musical genre of rap. In a *New
York Times* op-ed article a few years ago the literary critic Henry Louis
Gates explained the alleged obscenity of the rap group 2 Live Crew by
arguing that the sexual explicitness of the group's music is a way of
countering stereotypes about black sexuality by using the language of
exaggeration that is common in black slang. One could expand on
Gates's argument and maintain that both rap music and black slang are
driven by a need to counter the public silencing that African Americans
have had to endure. In rap the aim seems to be to keep speaking at all
costs, as if to stop is to leave oneself vulnerable and undefined. It does
with black male ghetto speech what Walker and Morrison do with
black Southern rural speech and what Roth and other first-generation
Jewish writers did with the speech of the Jewish shtetl. They carry a private, unsanctioned, and once powerless discourse into a public realm,
insisting through sheer chutzpah and in-your-face assertiveness that
this discourse is worth attending to. Ironically, the censorship furor
surrounding certain rap lyrics reenacts the dynamic behind the music.
For the very idea of censorship becomes a signifier for a history of being
silenced, and it is a resistance to being silenced that fuels the music in
the first place.

I am a beneficiary of these inroads against silence. As a woman who has
lived through the women's movement, I can invoke some of the same
tendencies in my speech and writing that I have described in the work
of Jews and African Americans. As I have grown older, I have become
more garrulous in public. It is not that I have learned proper argu-
mentative techniques and can speak like a man. It is, rather, that I can
to carry on my public arguments in the same style that I do my private
ones. I am less ashamed of emotional riffs and choppy transitions. This

is both a function of the confidence that comes with age and of the more general fact that, like other minorities, I can use my public speech to register past repression because public space now provides an opening. This opening has been won through the efforts of the civil rights and women's movements, but it is also, perhaps, the result of a certain lack of vigilance on the part of the mainstream American male. As James anticipated in his novel more than a century ago, male reticence is very glamorous, but it doesn't make for a pragmatic defense against the wily foreigner who, by dexterity or filibustering—by the sheer ability to fill space with fighting or feeling words—can win the day.

Freedom of speech was amended to the Constitution as the first of the Bill of Rights in 1791. Yet that freedom, set down as a mere right, cannot address the complexity of what it means to speak freely. For the assumption of this freedom is not a matter of simply lifting a constraint. It is, rather, a slow erosion of conventional barriers separating the public and private spheres, making it possible for those outsiders to the American establishment to speak in their own voice within it. As this process has come about, it has inspired a change in the very nature of public speech. No longer does the message pretend to stand univocally for some promised or potential action; it is now concerned as well with delivering the context and character of the speaker.

Of course, there is a certain danger inherent in the empowerment of private speech. This is the danger of losing the reciprocity that Henry James understood to be basic to communication—of devolving into a cacophonous battle of competing discourses. The compartmentalization of speech and silence, of private and public, has been eroded in our culture. What seems to be needed now is an oscillation between speech and silence in both spheres, a taking turns so as to learn and borrow from the discourses of others—an exchange rather than a simple enunciation of personal meaning. Where once one group spoke and others were consigned to silence, now perhaps we can create a society in which each has a chance to speak and thus can also find strength and equanimity in silence.

Rx for Premature Labor: Reading Trollope

*L*ATE one night, when I was only twenty-six weeks pregnant with my second child, I began to experience the slow, relatively painless but quite perceptible contractions that were familiar to me as the signs of labor. I knew that twenty-six weeks was too soon to have a baby, and I was in a state of mild alarm by the time I left for the hospital. It was close to one o'clock in the morning when my husband and I hurried onto the Labor and Delivery floor. If I had been worried on the way in, the scene on that floor hardly calmed me. Screaming women in bathrobes, their young children clinging to their knees, crowded the corridor, and overworked nurses and aides were rushing in and out of rooms with bedpans and blood-stained linen. I caught only an occasional glimpse of a disheveled physician padding in or out of a delivery room in a green pajamalike outfit and the little elastic cap that the women in the school cafeteria used to wear. There was a din of pain, anger, and confusion on that floor, an air of mayhem that I am told is not uncommon in urban hospitals during certain peak periods.

I was shepherded to a small cubicle of a room at the end of the floor, arranged on an uncommonly narrow bed that seemed nonetheless to take up all available space, and hooked up to an IV after a few unsuccessful but bloody stabs by an intern (the nurses usually did this, he said, but they were all busy with a really difficult delivery down the hall). He told me that the IV would pump what was necessary into me. There were, he explained, his eyes blinking with fatigue behind his thick glasses, a series of conventional steps that would be followed in a case like mine. They would start by trying to hydrate me: a simple saline solution pumped into the veins often did the trick—"stopped the labor in its tracks," as he put it. Despite the fact that the contractions had grown more frequent and more intense, the intern's words were vaguely reassuring. I was not then in what is referred to as "active labor"; he had made the treatment seem routine; and he had sketched out such an array of alternative remedies that I felt sure that medical technology would soon solve my problem. And so my husband went home to relieve the neighbor we had called in to stay with our five-year-old, who was dreaming peacefully under his poster of Superman, oblivious to our absence.

There followed eight infernal hours. As it turned out, the Labor and Delivery floor was operating at maximum capacity that night and was staffed by only two residents and the young intern, who had been working already for twenty-four hours straight. My room was located at the end of the corridor across from the laundry room, to which a steady stream of orderlies, talking loudly, came and went with bundles of laundry that they threw, with what seemed to me unnecessary aggression, down a rattling metal chute. I could not reach the rope that summoned the nurse without bringing on another contraction. Despite the reassurances I had received, the labor hadn't stopped. As the hours passed, I had graduated through the drugs that the intern had recited to us earlier in the evening, and I was now on a very high dose of something that greatly increased my heart rate and blood pressure, causing me to sweat profusely. The room, barely large enough to contain its racklike bed, was crowded on one side with the IV equipment and on the other with the monitor, a dreadful contraption that recorded on a rolling piece of graph paper the inexorable rise and fall of each contraction. How can I describe the terror that that machine came to inspire in me? It stood there, waiting to indict me, as I began to feel the slow, almost imperceptible but, to my heightened nerves, terribly evident pull of the abdomen that marked the beginning of a contraction. Once underway the contraction was destined to follow a certain course, and I came to know, from the first small twinge, just how intense it was likely to be, how long it would extend itself across the graph paper, and how high its peak would rise on the light-blue cross-hatching. I knew that to give birth to the baby now would be a probable disaster, and I wanted more than anything to relax my gradually tightening muscles. But I was helpless to control this stubborn physical drive. The monitor, with its rolling graph paper, became imbued for me with a taunting, malevolent character, literally rubbing my face in the proof that my condition was getting worse.

All I know is that after hours and hours of lying there I became stricken with a desperation so great that it seemed in itself to be causing the contractions to gallop through my body. Close to dawn a new resident finally came on duty—a young woman with soft gray eyes and the refreshing look of someone who had just had a good night's sleep and a shower. I beseeched her for help, and whether she had some insight into my condition or was operating by instinct, she responded immediately by giving me a shot of morphine, enough to put me into a deep, dreamless slumber. When I awoke the contractions had slowed.

But my sense of panic did not subside. When I tried to explain to my husband and parents, who arrived soon after, what had happened and why I was still in a state bordering on frenzy, they could not grasp my mood. I had had a difficult night, they understood; fortunately, the labor had been brought under control. Why, then, didn't I calm down, especially as I kept explaining to them that I thought the state of my nerves was linked to the state of my muscles?

But this was precisely the point. From early in the evening before I had made a dim connection between my mind and my body, a connection of seeming inconsequence to the medical personnel, with the possible exception of the gray-eyed resident (who, like so many others I had seen that night, had disappeared, never to be seen again). The irony, of course, was that the more I tried to will myself to relax, the more my body stiffened and resisted, and the more intense the labor became. And, as each new contraction heightened my terror, the cycle repeated itself. It was a case of what systems engineers have termed "escalating positive feedback"—but I was the escalating system, and I was not equipped with a means of short-circuiting my internal machinery. Indeed, any action I took to de-escalate what was going on seemed only to feed into the already existing cycle of pain and stress. I felt myself in the position of having the whole force of my desire work against the very thing that that desire aimed at.

If engineering offered one reading of my situation, religion offered another. During the whole of my ordeal I knew that religion could manage my case in a way that scientific knowledge could not. I am not a religious person, but I have read about religious ideas and about characters influenced by religious ideas. What was needed was a relinquishing of the will, a giving up of the struggle. This I had gropingly done when I had called to the resident for help, but I still had weeks ahead of me in which I wanted my will to be quiescent, and I felt that taking too much in the way of morphine or Valium might harm the baby. It was then that I understood why people read the Bible. My grandmother in old age had been nursed by a woman who read the Bible morning, noon, and night, to the great puzzlement of my family. What, we used to wonder, did she find to engross her? As she was not an articulate woman (or perhaps felt no need to be one), she never told us. I had always been struck by the quaintness of the convention that left Bibles in hotel rooms. I couldn't imagine that anyone actually turned to them for late night reading. But, ever since that harrowing night on the Labor floor, I see Bible reading differently. An analysis of biblical style by the German literary critic Erich Auerbach that I had read in graduate school and have since gone back to reread now carries enormous power in the wake of my experience with premature labor. Auerbach makes the point that the Bible subordinates everything to its premise: the premise that it is true, if not in the literal sense, then in the much more domineering spiritual sense. "The Scripture stories," he writes, "do not . . . court our favor, they do not flatter us that they may please us and enchant us—they seek to subject us, and if we refuse to be subjected we are rebels." And he continues by explaining that the Bible is "fraught with 'background' and mysterious, containing a second, concealed meaning . . . we are to fit our own life into its world, feel ourselves to be elements in its structure of universal history." Reading the Bible as a believer is to efface desire and disappointment by sinking into background and into mystery.

Auerbach then contrasts the biblical style with the Greek epic style of Homer, which, he says, has precisely the opposite goal, to "court" "flatter" "please" and "enchant." In Homer's poetry nothing is subordinated; all elements contribute to a design that makes no pretense of being true but seeks, rather, to create its own vibrant, entertaining reality—to create, that is, a dazzling surface by which we as readers can, in Auerbach's words, "be made to forget our own reality for a few hours."

What Auerbach has done is to sketch out the two alternatives open to the thwarted, suffering will: one can bury oneself in faith or find refuge in imaginative escape. I know that in my moment of most intense suffering I would have liked to have been able to lose myself in a religious text. But I had neither the temperament nor the training to do so and had to settle for the temporary oblivion offered by imaginative literature.

Finding the literature that could do this for me, however, was in itself no easy task. For literature is not always, not even often, calming.

Auerbach had suggested that Homer could beguile, but I had no patience for the remoteness of his world or for the ethos of war and heroism that defined its boundaries. But when I turned to more contemporary books, they either did not hold me or they upset me, precisely what I wished to avoid. Well-meaning visitors to my hospital room had brought me best-sellers, "good urban books," as they called them: a novel by Tom Wolfe about New York corruption and a police suspense novel about a big-city DA suspected of killing a female DA who had been his lover. Both of these books had been wildly hyped, and I had been assured that I wouldn't be able to put them down, but I found both unreadable—the caricatured nastiness of the one and the unrelenting squalor of the other seemed to go straight to my stomach and upset it terribly. When I turned to the books I had always loved to read and write about—mostly nineteenth-century novels and poetry— I found myself suffering a different kind of anxiety. For these books were tainted by their association with the effort of work. I could not read them without thinking about them, and, when I thought, my will exerted itself and began to turn upon my condition and rile my nerves and my muscles.

My mother sought relaxing alternatives; she purchased stacks of fashion magazines: *Vogue*, *Elle*, and *Mademoiselle* (whose titles alone evoke an idea of femininity free of the burdens of real life) and the more low-brow self-help mags, those curiosities that seem to be able to reconcile the most traditional edicts about femininity with some of the more radical possibilities of lifestyle: pink out-of-focus ads for feminine deodorant placed opposite articles about women living in hardy isolation in the Adirondacks. I have always found the tolerance of these magazines appealing—if you want to go hiking in four-inch heels, for example, they will back you all the way. But for my present condition they offered no solace. I needed to be embraced by an all-encompassing alternative reality, and the magazines, like the TV game shows and sitcoms that I tried to watch, were little patchwork pieces. They did not define a world and hence had no ability to fasten me to them. My mind wandered from their stylish pages to the frightfulness of my condition and wouldn't go back.

I don't know how long it took me to find what I wanted. Only a day or two, I tend to think, but by that time I had sampled many potential remedies. Books and magazines were strewn around the hospital

room, and I was hooked up to a set of relaxation tapes in which a seductive female voice talked about "letting it all go" over a background of
breaking waves. I had even been visited by a motley group of staff psy-
chiatrists, most of whom were more interested in talking about
whether they would ever be taken seriously by other doctors than
about my case, which they seemed to dismiss as a case of yuppie
malaise akin to their own career anxiety. Finally, however, I did find
what I was looking for. I found a more contemporary Homer, my own
secular scripture. I found Trollope.

Anthony Trollope was an enormously prolific, moderately
renowned British novelist of the Victorian period. Although I have
made my search seem arduous and extensive, I should say that hitting
upon Trollope as I did was nothing short of miraculous. There was no
rational explanation for why I should decide to read him. He fell within
the period that I was supposed to know well as a teacher and scholar of
nineteenth-century literature, but to my mild shame I had never really
read him. Oh, I had skimmed a few volumes here and there in college
and had not been impressed. He seemed to me (though I can't claim to
have originated this assessment) to be a poor man's Jane Austen, without her wit, her stylistic grace, or her profundity. He wrote about eccle-
siastical and political subjects that were intimately entwined with the
events of his day (Austen, to her credit as I always thought, had no such
sense of topicality). His novels seemed to go on forever. He had written
forty-seven of them, and the bulk of these were parts of two series—
family sagas with vast casts of characters, some of whom cropped up
again and again, sometimes in leading, sometimes in supporting roles.
One series, known popularly as the Barchester novels, dealt with the
domestic and professional goings-on among the clerical hierarchy of a
British country parish; the other series, known as the Palliser novels,
dealt with the same kinds of matter, this time as it concerned a political
elite and their hangers-on. God knows why I even thought of Trollope
in my hospital bed. But, once I did, I became convinced that he would
serve my purposes, that he would take me gently into his world and
keep me there for as long as I needed (forty-seven novels, after all—one
doesn't run out quickly).

And so, for three weeks, propped on my left side (the uterus is less
strained if one lies on the left side), I read Trollope. I read through the
Barchester novels, book by book, sending my husband out to comb the

libraries and bookstores, for I was determined to read in order, then, moving on to the Palliser novels. At 3 a.m., when the nurses changed shifts and the Benadryl taken at 11 had worn off, I opened to the dog-eared page of *Doctor Thorne*; and at 9 a.m., as they wheeled in the monitor, the contraption that still made me tremble, I was already well into *Framely Parsonage*. I read over the lunch tray and opened a book as soon as a visitor left the room. And I was clutching *The Duke's Children* (the last of the Palliser novels) as I was wheeled into the delivery room at thirty-seven weeks.

Now that I am done with that ordeal and delivered of a healthy baby—now that I have reentered a life in which panic is not lurking in the hall, waiting to be rolled in with the monitor—I no longer need Trollope. But I have developed a sentimental attachment to the idea of him and have sought to find specific reasons for the calming effect he had on me. Thus, I open at random, and I find a passage like the following, in the first novel in the Barchester series:

> My readers will guess from what I have written that I myself do not like Mr. Slope, but I am constrained to admit that he is a man of parts. He knows how to say a soft word in the proper place; he knows how to adapt his flattery to the ears of his hearers; he knows the wiles of the serpent, and he uses them. Could Mr. Slope have adapted his manners to men as well as to women, could he ever have learnt the ways of a gentleman, he might have risen to great things.

The passage is quintessential Trollope. Note the ease and egalitarian spirit of the authorial intrusion. This author, unlike a George Eliot or a Thackeray, in no way pretends to be a better or a wiser man than his reader. There is nothing strenuous or didactic about his narrative voice. The intrusion is largely gratuitous; its function is to be reassuring. We don't like Mr. Slope—he has been painted as a vile creature for many pages already—but it is nice to have the author tell us that he doesn't like him either. Nor is this the only genial service the paragraph per-forms. For, while the author grants Mr. Slope a certain wily power, he also proceeds to assure us that there is no need to worry, the man is not destined to triumph. Again, we don't really have to be told this—the

conventions of the genre serve to cue us in to the fact that such an unsa-
vory character will be foiled in the end—but Trollope, bless him, must
hammer home his point and put us completely at our ease: don't worry
about Mr. Slope, he reassures us, he'll get his comeuppance. Finally, the
paragraph implies that there is a social system in place that will bring
Mr. Slope to justice. It suggests that, though this man can insinuate
himself into the good graces of the ladies, he is not so adept with men,
and, what is perhaps even more telling against him, he does not have
the manners of a gentleman.

In short, the paragraph asserts obliquely that masculine judgment
and social class both operate as part of a system of checks on base and
cunning characters like Mr. Slope. As a feminist, this should offend me,
and it does when I read it as I do now in a moment of calm reflection.
However, reading Trollope in a hospital bed in a state of panic, one
doesn't weigh doctrine. And, indeed, it is not so much sexism that operates in Trollope's world as it is a sexual order that cooperates in a general sense of orderliness. For his novelistic world is constructed out of a
respect for a conventional order, out of maxims and hierarchies and traditional rites and ceremonies. He plays around with some of these, as
when, in the Palliser novels, he has the delightful but not well-born
Phineas Finn make his way through the thicket of the political system
and, through precisely the kind of ingratiation with women that he
says won't work with Mr. Slope, does make it near to the top. He allows
this favored character a certain insouciant mobility, but he does so with
a clear sense of the special dispensation he is giving his character.
Phineas Finn has been chosen as a hero, endowed with extraordinary
doses of charm and luck, and made as clean and upright as one could
wish. Trollope moves Phineas about as my son moves one of his super-
heroes, but the landscape in which Trollope moves his character is not
a fantastic one; it is a world constructed very carefully out of the pieces
that we take to be social reality. There is nothing threatening or surprising about it.

Ultimately, what I came to see about Trollope—what had beguiled
me in my hospital bed and seemed less than compelling once I was out
of it—was that he was the consummate *daydreamer*. I suppose all imaginative art has an element of daydream—Freud argued this in one of
his essays on creativity. But I think that great writers are not principally
daydreamers. They engage with the world as they see it: they in some

way do battle with it and transform it in a deep as well as a surface sense. By contrast, the whole thrust of Trollope's art was *not* to change the world but, rather, to win imaginatively on the battlefield of life as he conceived it actually to be. Hence, he does not critique social roles or stereotypes; he makes them work for the characters he likes and against the characters he doesn't like. Slope will not succeed because "men"— that is, men like Trollope—will sniff him out, and his bad manners will disgrace him in the end. Slope exists in the novel like the types my husband angrily remembers from college, whom he knew to be sneaky and disrespectful of women and whom he hated all the more because he resented their romantic successes. Trollope uses his fiction to wreak vengeance on the type. By the same token he takes a charming, well-intentioned young man and makes him surmount all the obstacles that society has to offer. Phineas Finn's story is a wish fulfillment, a daydream about success; Finn is decked out in the finest imaginary characteristics and given all the best chances to shine. In reading that novel, whether one is a man or a woman, one is drawn unconsciously to see oneself as Phineas Finn—to repeat the daydream that the author had when he wrote the novel.

There is to Trollope's life all the ingredients likely to produce an inveterate daydreamer. He was the neglected son of two distracted parents. His father was a financial failure and an alcoholic; his mother, Frances Trollope, was an extraordinarily energetic and unsentimental woman, who left Anthony when he was still in his teens to travel with a more favored son to the United States to set up a department store. The venture failed, but she returned to write about her experiences and become famous in England as a travel writer and essayist. Meanwhile, Anthony was sent to boarding school, where he was maligned for being poor and unfashionable. Although he eventually married and earned acclaim as a writer, he never seemed to gain the respect from his family or from himself that one would have expected. He continued throughout his long life to churn out novels at a rate rarely seen before or since, writing every day for a set number of hours. It is an index to his self-image that, when he got around to writing his autobiography, he did irreperable damage to his reputation for posterity by admitting that he approached his work with the same attitude as a carpenter.

This admission seems to me perfectly in keeping with the guilelessness of the daydreamer. It also contains part of the key to why the novels were so appealing to me. Daydreams do not entail intellectual work; they are escapes from such work. They reflect a relaxing of the will, a letting go of what Freud would call "the reality principle," at the same time that they are permeated with the world's premises, prejudices, and codes. They are so easy on both the writer and the reader precisely because they do not require either a literal leap out of this world, as science fiction or fantasy does, or a metaphorical leap, as strenuous moral novels like those of Tolstoy or George Eliot do. Trollope takes us to a familiar landscape and places us in a position of watching our daydream self triumph and our daydream enemy fail. When good people die in Trollope, as the old bishop does at the beginning of *Barchester Towers* or even as the lovely Glencora Palliser does toward the end of the Palliser series, they fade away. When someone is particularly egregious in a noncomic way, he may die more violently—Slope is too much a caricature of the hypocritcal prelate to be killed off—but Frederic Lopez in *The Prime Minister* throws himself under a train. Here, however, the character has become impossibly tedious, and his death seems the only plot device available to set his wife free to marry the man she is destined for. Even when violence happens, it happens as it does in daydream: it serves as a means of bringing the protagonist closer to what he or she wants. Nothing wrenches or tears; nothing touches below the surface. One is carried on the current of plot, lulled by the assurance that one's expectations about people and events will be fulfilled in due time. Indeed, taking one's time to arrive at a foreordained conclusion is part of the pleasure of daydream. Trollope does have his magnificent moments—moments when he takes a character, as he sometimes does with Mr. Slope or Lizzie Eustace in the *Eustace Diamonds*—and plays out that character's foibles with a vitality that approaches the inspired excess of Dickens. Nonetheless, I always got the feeling that these characterizations were Trollope's way of getting back at some school bully or some pretty girl who snubbed him during those terrible days at Harrow.

And, yet, I must end by admitting that I am puzzled. I had read a great deal of Trollope by the time my baby was finally born, and I left the hospital comfortable in my assessment of his writing. Then I was thrown for a loop when, recently, I picked up *He Knew He Was Right*, which suddenly appeared on the shelf of the university store. I found myself in unfamiliar territory. In this late Trollope novel the protagonist is a husband driven insane by the force of his jealousy as it is fed by the stubborn pride of his wife. The atmosphere in the Italian scenes is claustrophobic, the style harsh and clotted, the writing intensely powerful. The effect is something like Shakespearean tragedy. That novel would have upset me had I read it during my hospitalization. But then, perhaps, I might have read it differently—assimilated it to my need for a certain kind of Trollope. As I consider this, the suspicion that I might have missed something in this author is superseded by the greater suspicion that I may have found in him only what I wanted to find. This suspicion is so unsettling that I have yet to return to Trollope for a fresh reading.

The Marriage Plot

*A*FTER I got married, I looked around and realized that I had entered a terrain where literature did not go.

My role models had always been the heroines of nineteenth-century novels by Fanny Burney, Jane Austen, Charlotte Brontë, and Elizabeth Gaskell: unmarried girls whose personal worth was tested as they made their way to the final reward of a good marriage. From these novels I learned the ins and outs of the courtship plot. I learned about the dangers of flattery and the pain of jilting; about the importance of civility and the necessity of honesty; about the value of friendship and the mistake of fortune hunting. I also learned to find beauty in the odd-looking physiognomy; depths of interest in the depressive personality; and passionate intensity in boorish manners (which I called awkward shyness or manly directness, depending on the circumstances). The cues that I had taken from the novels of courtship kept the experience intense and interesting—gave texture and moral weight to that long stretch of dating years in my twenties. During those years I might have acted foolishly or been hurt through my own misreading, but I was always part of the plot, and the plot was purposeful: it led to the good marriage.

Once there, however, what to do? The novels that had brought me to this point unceremoniously shut the door. Marriage in nineteenth-century fiction happened in the last pages, suggesting that the heroines' lives as heroines ended with the ceremony. And, if a marriage didn't happen, the heroine usually died—the fate of such luminaries in the tradition as Clarissa Harlowe, Catherine Earnshaw, and Maggie Tulliver. It doesn't take great astuteness to see the structural relationship between marriage and death operating here. Carolyn Heilbrun in her consideration of the subject twenty years ago literalized the equation. "For the woman before modern times, marriage is," she writes, "except in rare instances, a kind of death. It is the death of her individual identity, the death of her person under law, her sexual sacrifice, . . . perhaps her literal death in childbirth." This is cogent social criticism, but it is, after all, referring to another time. One would imagine that more modern novels would amend the equation and find room to represent love, friendship, and personal growth within marriage.

Unfortunately, this doesn't happen; fiction fails to rise to the occasion, or sees no occasion to rise to. George Eliot propels a number of her heroines into marriages early in her novels and explores the disappointments and cruelties of those relationships. Good marriages, when she includes them, she continues to relegate to the end, just as Jane Austen did. Her successors, protomodernists such as George Gissing and George Meredith, far from rescuing marriage, sink courtship—demonstrating in case after case that the passage to marriage is more of a mercenary or desperate venture than a self-improving one. Thomas Hardy, D. H. Lawrence, and Henry James are deeply skeptical of the marriage plot, and when they draw back the curtain on married life tend to reveal a depressing spectacle in which men and women quietly prey on each other or, more viciously, rip each other apart. In modern women's fiction marriage tends to be represented in the most ambivalent terms. Virginia Woolf's heroines are wary and doubting about marriage; Jean Rhys's, masochistic in their marital choices; Doris Lessing's, neurotic; the heroines of Barbara Pym and Anita Brookner, cosmically resigned to a state of dismal solitude. It would seem from any survey of modern literature that authors were intent on dashing the expectations of readers like me who were bred on the courtship plot. The institution, so carefully guarded and idealized in the earlier fiction, is revealed in the later to be a false Eden, a moral and aesthetic wasteland.

Those of us who have been married for any duration know this not to be true. Good marriages do exist. Though they are not idylls, neither are they wastelands. Good marriages are leavened by their share of unhappiness, irritation, and discontent as well as joy, peace, and achievement. But unhappiness, when tempered by happiness, when not given lease to escalate into adultery, divorce, or murder, is simply not good grist for fictional narrative as we have come to know it. The equation of marriage with a woman's death, noted earlier, holds the key to the issue. Although Carolyn Heilbrun is right to derive a social critique from this equation as it applies to the premodern period, her reading is not altogether valid even for that time. After all, we have diaries and letters indicating that, despite the inequities of custom and law, many women of the nineteenth century and before had relationships of intimacy and friendship with their husbands. It is novelistic fiction that could find no place for these aspects of relationship, and the reason seems to be less a function of the institution of marriage than of fictional narrative itself.

For the bias of narrative is to equate its own ending and the silence that ensues with death; and where the courtship plot is the dominant structure (and the powerful conditioning of the courtship plot looms over modern novels as well as nineteenth-century ones), this is to equate marriage with death. Once we acknowledge this, we can begin to understand more fully why the equation is false. The end of narrative is the place where life gets lived, whereas the narrative is only where it gets talked about. Jane Austen, the great practitioner of the courtship plot, seems to have been aware of this when it came to writing the conclusion of *Mansfield Park*. In announcing the heroine's success in finally winning the affections of the hero, now that he has been freed from the clutches of another woman, she explains:

> I purposely abstain from dates on this occasion, that every one may be at liberty to fix their own, aware that the cure of unconquerable passion, and the transfer of unchanging attachments, must vary much as to time in different people.—I only intreat every body to believe that exactly at the time when it was quite natural that it should be so, and not a week earlier, Edmund did cease to care about Miss Crawford, and became as anxious to marry Fanny, as Fanny herself could desire.

Austen lets it be known that she has not only reached the end of her narrative but also reached the place where narrative no longer has a function. In a sense *Mansfield Park* is an exception in the Austen canon in that it really isn't about courtship in the usual sense. It is about a wrongheaded courtship—that of Edmund of Mary Crawford. Alongside that courtship there has existed the relationship of Edmund and Fanny, a relationship more like a marriage in its steady affection than anything we tend to see in nineteenth-century English novels. This may be why Austen formally unites Edmund and Fanny by invoking the formula of courtship in a satirical way. The formula, she appears to be implying, isn't appropriate to a real relationship, only to a novelistic one.

Phyllis Rose, in her book *Parallel Lives: Five Victorian Marriages*, points out that two of the relationships she discusses (that of George Eliot and George Henry Lewes and of John Stuart Mill and Harriet Taylor) were unusually happy but did not fit the mold of a romantic plot. Eliot and Lewes were unable to formally marry (his wife would not grant him a divorce), but despite the potential drama of their situation (and the fact that many of their contemporaries saw fit to snub them for impropriety), they were not strident in their union; they were, on the contrary, self-effacing and rather conventional. Mill and Taylor, for their part, turned on their head the conventional power relations of the couple: he deferred to her judgment; she was not shy about asserting her opinion on everything, including his work. But their unorthodox behavior hardly looked bold or dramatic, and it won them more ridicule than admiration. Both of these marriages seem to have avoided the expected without explicitly embracing the unexpected. Rose points out that the plots we think are appropriate to given situations are often restrictive and artificial and that marriages work when they can escape that straitjacket in subtle but profound ways.

But Tolstoy's statement about the sameness of happy families (and by extension happy marriages) is true to the extent that there is something unnarratable, and hence undistinctive, about a good marriage, which may be the point of the whole venture. It may be that one enters marriage when one feels oneself exhausted by plot. Certainly, one can impose a plot on married life: one can talk of the early years, the years with children, the years of financial strain, the later years of a renewed closeness, and so forth. But somehow these landmarks, these narrative junctures, seem artificial and irrelevant. Marriage happens not in these plotted points but in the stretches of noise, repetition, and sameness.

Go to a playground some weekday afternoon and listen to the mothers there talk about their children. What you hear are some discussions about how the children are doing developmentally (subjects such as first steps, drinking from a cup, toilet training, etc.), some exchanges about cute behavior, and some trading of pediatric advice. What is going on is an oral antihistory, a kind of anti-Homeric epic. These stories have no continuity; they don't make points or have real conclusions; they are musings, vignettes, pieces of the puzzle of child-hood. Marriage can be compared to child rearing in that it too exists representationally as an oral antihistory. It lurks in the unassuming pockets of daily discourse: it can be glimpsed in the tone of letters, in the anecdotes that one partner relates about the other in a diary entry, in the casual dropping of the other's name and the unconscious appro-priation of the other's turn of phrase or opinion in conversation.

It is perhaps no coincidence, given its problems with representa-tion, that marriage, like child rearing, has spawned a vast prescriptive literature. Psychologists and other, often dubious experts extrapolate from the patterns of bad marriages they've seen or from the successes of their own relationships to produce a patchwork model that readers can dip into for advice on such issues as "how to fight more produc-tively" or "how to reprogram your sex life." These efforts at represen-tation, makeshift and shallow though they tend to be, are testimony that the good marriage has at least a potential existence in the public imagination.

One genre that makes a more profound attempt at representing the good marriage is that of biography and memoir. Here the advantage of retrospect is able to present friction and disillusionment on the one hand and intimacy and shared achievement on the other so as to relay something of the balance of difficulty and ease that characterizes a good marriage. Yet it would seem that one has to be outside of the mar-riage looking back at it (either personally, one spouse being dead, or historically, as the chronicler of someone else's marriage), for this per-spective to be rendered. Phyllis Rose, as I have mentioned, was able to do this by studying a number of Victorian marriages. Nigel Nicolson was able to do it in describing the marriage of his parents, Vita Sackville-West and Harold Nicolson—a marriage that, for all its eccen-tricities and infidelities, was, according to the son, a success. Diana Trilling was able to do it in her memoir of her marriage to Lionel Trilling. Although she doesn't spare references to her husband's lacer-ating black moods or her bouts of paranoia, the overall impression, as surveyed from the distance at which she writes (her husband dead now twenty years), is of a relationship in which the bad parts were detours into narrative in an otherwise unplotted, but loving, union. Both Nicol-son and Trilling seem intent on describing difficulties of the marriages in question less for their intrinsic interest than as a means of setting off the larger point; that the marriages worked in the face of these difficulties. "If their marriage is seen as a harbour," writes Nicolson of his parents, "their love affairs were mere ports of call. It was to the harbour that each returned; it was there that both were based."

Ironically, the genre that manages to represent directly what Nicolson can only describe metaphorically is the television sitcom. The good marriage has been represented on TV since the beginning of the medium through a string of couples: Ozzie and Harriet, Ralph and Alice, Lucy and Desi, Ward and June, Archie and Edith, and Roseanne and Dan come to mind as noteworthy examples. Although these shows rely on narrative incidents that often involve disagreements and misunderstandings between husband and wife, the presentation softens and attenuates all crises through the use of running jokes and farcical situations and through the simple fact that the shows return, week after week, the relationships intact. The shows are predicated upon a quality of repetition that captures the "feel" of married life: each week the same brief and pleasant scenario is replayed at the beginning—a starting point and anchor for the action, a "harbour" to which the partners will always, despite the manic activity that follows, be brought back. In this sense sitcoms contain a built-in homeostatic mechanism: the fact that the family must return to normal at the end of each week's show (hence, Ralph's often concluding remark: "Alice, you're the greatest!"). The overriding sense one gets from these shows is that nothing really happens; the couple is engulfed by action and noise but remains impervious, stolid, unchanged in the face of it. This is a simplified truth about the good marriage, for, as the partners change and as life changes around them, the couple itself remains. It is the given within which all action, including individuality, swirls and is, though often painfully and unevenly, assimilated.

This may be why, even in the forms of representation I have mentioned, there is always the sense that what makes the marriage work is unrepresentable. What is good in the good marriage shows itself only indirectly and can only be glimpsed when the focus lies elsewhere: on situations and events in which the couple is simply called upon to operate *as* a couple. For this reason some of the most successful renderings of the couple have been in the genre of the suspense novel and film—one thinks of Harriet Vane and Peter Wimsey and of Nick and Nora Charles—in which the life of the good marriage supports the working out of an intricate plot that occupies the foreground of the action.

Perhaps one could say that the good in a good marriage is inaccessible to representation because it depends on what Keats called "negative capability"—the art of not trying too hard and not asserting oneself too much. It is that part of the marriage that chooses not to be seen or heard, that is modest, unassuming, content with a secondary part. It occurs when each partner stops wanting to write the marriage plot as though it were a continuation of the courtship plot and is content to live as Ozzie and Harriet rather than as Anna Karenina and Count Vronsky.

At the conclusion of Dickens's *Little Dorrit*, Amy Dorrit and Arthur Clennam, weary soldiers in life's battle, finally marry and "descend," in Dickens's words, into the "roaring streets, inseparable and blessed; and as they passed along in sunshine and shade, the noisy and the eager, and the arrogant and the froward and the vain, fretted and chafed, and made their usual uproar." Looking from the outside in, as conditioned by the courtship plot, one is liable to find the prospect of descending into that uncharted territory, into those "roaring streets," less than compelling. But this seems precisely what Dickens had in mind when he referred to his characters' journey as a descent. It is a grateful throwing off of the exertions of courtship, of the demands of personality, and of the exigencies of plot. One must have had one's share of purposeful narrative, one must like one's partner, one must want not just the idea but the reality of "happily ever after."

Born to Shop

"*I* DON'T care anything about his house," said Isabel.

"That is very crude of you. When you have lived as long as I, you will see that every human being has his shell, that you must take the shell into account. By the shell I mean the whole envelope of circumstances. There is no such thing as an isolated man or woman; we are each of us made up of a cluster of appurtenances. What do you call one's self? Where does it begin? Where does it end? It overflows into everything that belongs to us—and then it flows back again. I know that a large part of myself is in the dresses I choose to wear. I have a great respect for *things!* One's self—for other people—is one's expression of one's self; and one's house, one's clothes, the books one reads, the company one keeps—these things are all expressive. . . ."

"I don't agree with you," [Isabel] said. "I think just the other way. I don't know whether I succeed in expressing myself, but I know that nothing else expresses me. Nothing that belongs to me is any measure of me; on the contrary, it's a limit, a barrier, and a perfectly arbitrary one. Certainly, the clothes which, as you say, I choose to wear, don't express me; and heaven forbid they should!"

"You dress very well," interposed Madame Merle, skillfully.

"Possibly; but I don't care to be judged by that. My clothes may express the dress-maker, but they don't express me. To begin with, it's not my own choice that I wear them; they are imposed upon me by society."

"Should you prefer to go without them?" Madame Merle inquired, in a tone which virtually terminated the discussion.

In this passage from Henry James's *The Portrait of a Lady* Isabel Archer, the free-spirited and idealistic young heroine, is arguing with her older, more worldly-wise friend, Serena Merle, a woman who, as it turns out, will lure Isabel into a disastrous marriage to a fortune hunter. Given the plot, Madame Merle's argument in favor of "things" seems

intended as a gloss on her unscrupulous character, while Isabel's dec-
laration of independence from things seems the mark of her superiority—of her status as heroine. Yet reading the exchange out of context
and in the present circumstances of my life, I find it impossible to
reduce the two women's positions to so simple a moral polarity. For all
that the novel stacks the cards against her, Madame Merle is no straw
woman in this debate. Her argument—that things exert powerful
claims on us and are expressive of us—becomes, if not more alluring,
certainly more inescapable, the older one grows.

I did not always see the merits of Madame Merle's position. When
I first read *Portrait of a Lady* in high school, Isabel entirely captured my
loyalty. I too believed in the self as a transcendent idea. My parents, my
father in particular, seemed to share Madame Merle's more earthbound
views. My father was a great believer in society. He wanted me to host
parties, run for class president, and go to proms and pep rallies. I stub-
bornly refused to comply. I did not have a facility for these activities,
although I suppose, had I been assured of being popular and of making
the cheerleading team, I might have been more receptive. As it was, my
father's partisanship of activities to which I was not physically or tem-
peramentally suited gave me two options: I could try to meet his expectations and achieve, at best, an undistinguished success, or I could
decide not to pursue them with vehemence and excel in my ability to
refuse. There was never really any contest here. I sensed that my refusal
to be the social creature my father wished me to be would open up possibilities for self-expression that any attempt to please him would have
denied me. And, once I began to define myself through resisting his
wishes, the strategy took on a life of its own.

At school my behavior was shaped by what I wouldn't do. I
wouldn't laugh at what others considered to be funny; I wouldn't be
nice to the cute boys; I wouldn't sign yearbooks at graduation. I wasn't
particularly pleasant or fun to be around, but I had a profile; I set a
course. This stretched even to include my appearance. During a time
when most girls wore their hair ironed into long, silky panels, I cut
mine very short (what my mother's friends, in their effort to smooth
over all suggestion of deviance, cheerfully called a "pixie cut"). I also
insisted on dressing only in black. Black clothing, as I vaguely understood it then, was clothing that resisted its status as clothing—it had
metaphysical properties, indicating to the world that my body was

only the shadow of an idea of itself. As Isabel puts it: "I don't know whether I succeed in expressing myself, but I know that nothing else expresses me." She uses things to express her by arguing that they don't. A black wardrobe did something of the same for me.

What Isabel misses in the argument, and what I missed at the time I first read the novel and paraded through the school cafeteria in a black leotard, is that she could not emerge as a free-spirited, idealistic heroine were Madame Merle not there to serve as her antagonist. Likewise, my father's badgering, worldly goals were necessary to me in order to carve out a space of higher, purer aspirations. When, in mellower later life, he became far less sure of what was best for me or perhaps simply more resigned to the fact that I wasn't going to do what he promoted, my idea of myself grew a little ragged around the edges; it lost some of its clarity. I took to goading him, trying to get a rise. Where would I be if I couldn't define myself against his conventional ideas about what was worth doing? The critic Lionel Trilling seemed to have in mind something similar when he praised nineteenth-century novels for their commitment to "realism" (a commitment that he sadly saw to be on the wane in contemporary fiction). Without a belief in the material world that realism implies, he argued, idealism becomes impossible: "In the degree that the novel gave credence to the world while withholding its assent, it established the reality of the moral or spiritual success that is defined by the rejection of the world's values." In other words, the novel gives us a social reality against which we can define ourselves as better. If we accept this argument, then Madame Merle is a representative of the novel form itself, the true partisan and partner of the author, and a generative force for Isabel Archer quite as much as my father was a generative force for me. Trilling wrote that the critical spirit cut loose from the material world is worse than useless; it is self-annihilating. It is the death drive without its counterforce in the crass vitality of life.

Madame Merle seems to understand this when she pushes Isabel's logic to its limits and tries to expose her dependence upon the very things that she scorns. She tells Isabel that she dresses very well, and, when her young friend refuses to accept the compliment, she challenges her to make her protest a literal one: to go without clothes. It is a challenge that, given the terms of their debate, could not possibly be met. For to go naked, as Madame Merle suggests, would be to break

out of the abstract realm within which idealism flourishes and into a
mode of expression that no longer demands a staged debate with a
practical-minded other person. It is a masterful challenge on Madame
Merle's part; for, since Isabel cannot by definition meet it, it must effectively end the argument and give the older woman the last word.

But does Madame Merle win the argument? This is harder to say.
Reading the novel as an adolescent, I didn't think so. I didn't care who
got the last word. I knew that Isabel's persuasiveness had nothing to do
with logic—that her position didn't in fact exist *in* argument but outside it. Although Madame Merle's final challenge to Isabel that she go
without clothes might have seemed to some activist type of my generation (I am talking about the early 1970s now) to be worth rising to, to
Isabel's (and my) "purer" view, it seemed only crude and beside the
point. If Isabel were to allow her idea of herself to enter reality and
parade around naked, then she would be no better than Madame
Merle. Isabel didn't stoop to respond to her friend—she let the argument go—and for this I loved her. Indeed, a large part of the appeal of
The Portrait of a Lady to the adolescent imagination has to do with its
willingness to back Isabel despite or, rather, because of her inability to
show why she's worth supporting. Ultimately, we are expected to comprehend that her heroinism resides in something not present in any
attempt to define her but, instead, in something that resists, as she puts
it, all limits and barriers, including definition. How empowering for a
teenager, riddled as she is with self-doubt, to be told that she can be a
heroine despite not being popular or beautiful—despite not possessing
any of the conventional attributes of the storybook heroine.

Yet, rereading the novel now, I can't say that I believe as strongly in that
ineffable self that I once found so compelling. I am not so entirely
Isabel's partisan in the debate and have moments of great sympathy for
Madame Merle. I like her point about the interdependence of the self
with its environment: "There is no such thing as an isolated man or
woman. . . . What do you call one's self? Where does it begin? Where
does it end?" Far from sounding selfish and narrow, this portion of her
argument sounds quite progressive and delimiting. Gregory Bateson,
the anthropologist and communications theorist who became a fore-
runner of the ecology movement, made a similar point in an essay written in 1971. He wanted us to see how arbitrary and destructive were

our conventional ways of punctuating the world and for us to conceive of mind and body, of the human organism and its environment, as inextricably linked:

> If you ask anybody about the localization and boundaries of the self, these confusions are immediately displayed. Or consider a blind man with a stick. Where does the blind man's self begin? At the tip of the stick? At the handle of the stick? Or at some point halfway up the stick?

Unlike Bateson, however, Madame Merle doesn't rest in the ecological perspective. She invokes it in order to subvert it, for she understands interdependence only from the point of view of her own interests. Having suggested the possibility of a fluid, unboundaried self, she shifts to a personal, materialistic one: "I have great respect for *things!* One's self, for other people, is one's expression of one self." While Bateson is intent upon making us aware of context so as to free us from enslavement within a self-centered conception of reality, Madame Merle seems to imply that the "envelope of circumstances" that makes up our lives limits and fixes us, places us in its thrall. What makes her so dangerous to others is that in her acute understanding of the claims that things make on her she becomes entirely thing oriented. She cannot allow anyone who touches her to escape her acquisitiveness. People become to her like her dresses: immediately altered or discarded when they cease to be properly expressive of her—cease, that is, to minister to her needs.

Even when Madame Merle's argument turns overtly materialistic, however, I cannot condemn her in the way I once did. It is no longer possible for me to see Isabel's idealism as pure and Madame Merle's materialism as impure. For Isabel's resistance to Madame Merle seems parasitic to me now—exploitative in its moral superiority, spinning off of the older woman's experience. I have become suspicious of that part of myself that still indulges in idealistic rages while sitting comfortably in my suburban home with my healthy children, my good job, and my husband with his good job. Let me either sacrifice what I have or keep my mouth shut. The Madame Merles who have struggled and suffered more than I have to gain a foothold for themselves are life's social conservatives. If I am ashamed of the way my liberal sentiments jar with my lifestyle, they are proud of their lifestyle; they see it as their due.

They want to be judged by what they wear, where they live, whom they know. They are good at telling the people who clean their homes, care for their children, and prune their hedges just precisely how they want the job done and how much they are willing to pay. They believe that exchanging money for services is an unambiguous and wholly appropriate way of ordering their lives—and they extend the idea into every nook and cranny of their existence, purchasing, through various currency, all the "appurtenances" that make up their envelope of circumstances. Although I continue to share with Isabel a sense that human desires and relationships are more unmanageable than this, I have nonetheless a grudging respect for those who seem not to think so: who know what they want and who try to arrange their lives accordingly.

But Madame Merle's position takes on further resonance still if one goes beyond this reading of her as a social conservative, a woman intent upon identifying herself with the rewards that her labor and experience have brought her. The argument she offers Isabel also reveals something sad and vulnerable that is more a function of aging than of experience. For with the intimation of mortality that comes with age, "things" take on still another character: they become magical and protective. "Every human being has his shell," Madame Merle explains. This shell does nothing if not protect the self, buttressing it against the ravages of life and time. Why is it, after all, if not because of the need to build and reinforce this shell, that shopping becomes more alluring as a pastime the older one gets? There is a woman in my neighborhood who has a sign stuck to the rear window of her car that reads "Born to Shop," a proclamation to the world of a fate devoted to aimless acquisitiveness. Why and for what does she shop? Is it because the hunting for things obscures the sense of the fragility of her life and her imminent extinction?

Clothing takes on a special, fetish-like importance for women as they grow older not so much because it is the means by which they can make their bodies more alluring (most fashionable clothing doesn't even pretend to do this) but because clothes are things that can be literally pressed to the flesh, appended to the self so as to give it more substance, more texture, more durability, more life. The more expensive and voguish the garment, the more it is like a talisman. Madame Merle, in the hollowness that characterizes what we come to know of her life and history, was "born to shop." One imagines that she is a regular haunter of sales racks, squinting at herself, draped in some drastically reduced designer garment in Loehmann's communal changing rooms.

Anita Brookner, a novelist with an extraordinarily developed imagination of vulnerability and despair, seems particularly attuned to the way women, as they age, grow addicted to the acquisition and arrangement of things. In Brookner's novel *The Misalliance* her heroine spends hours getting dressed and coiffed, turning herself out impeccably to meet the long bright hours of the day, hours that she must work to fill now that her husband has left her. Her carefully groomed appearance provides her with a protective shell that thwarts the pity and involvement of others, that keeps life, in all of its disorder and abrasiveness, at bay. On one outing she watches as the widows of the neighborhood, facsimiles of herself, emerge for their daily outing:

> Elderly, tired, and overdressed . . . Blanche saw stark and heavy colour applied to sagging cheeks and lips, patent leather shoes crammed on to plump and painful feet, hair golden and unnaturally swirled and groomed. Blanche watched a woman wearing a heavy fur coat feel for the edge of the pavement with her stick; a scaly hand, ornamented with long red nails and an accumulation of rings, emerged from the weighty sleeve like a small armadillo.

The image of the shell that Madame Merle employed as a metaphor for the things that envelop and express us is here represented as incongruous, unsightly, even threatening. If it expresses the self, it is a self ugly and ossified, ambulatory but dead.

When I read the exchange between Isabel and Madame Merle now, I am put off by both sides. I can understand and even sympathize with Madame Merle's argument, where once that was impossible, but I still cannot like it. It either denies the whole idea of a self or asserts it as an armored factotum, a selfish or pathetic aggregate of things that, even as it may express the self, also crushes it and those around it. Yet Isabel's opposition has only a fleeting charm for me now; it cannot be compelling to a mature mind. I cannot take her disregard for limits and barriers seriously, for I know that life abounds with real obstacles, and I know that she will be sunk by them by the end of the novel. As a healthier middle ground, I like my mother's stated philosophy. "There's

nothing wrong with liking things," she always told me, "just be prepared to give them up if you have to." A nice phrase. But easier said
than done. For what does "being prepared" mean? And how do you
test your preparedness? My mother now clings to her house, doesn't
want to move to a more easily cared for apartment, says she has too
many things that she likes, is accustomed to, depends upon, in that
house with its too many rooms now that the children have grown. The
thought of moving frightens and fatigues her.

James's later novel *The Spoils of Poynton* is a powerful tribute to
both the allure of things and the heroism of giving them up. With his
typical gift for making abstract moral choices seem vital and unassailable, he has his heroine survey a priceless collection of art objects that
might have been hers but which she has lost on principle and conclude
that "she thought of them without a question of any personal right."
Fleda Vetch, the heroine's unlikely name, goes on to express her satisfaction in her new, more modest surroundings. "If there were more
there would be too many to convey the impression in which half the
beauty resides [she explains to her friend]—the impression, somehow,
of something dreamed and missed, something sensibly gone. . . . Ah,
there's something here that will never be in the inventory!" In her scorn
for inventory she joins Isabel Archer as an exemplar of the antimateri-
alist heroine.

And yet I wonder whether such a heroine could only have been
created by a man. Eloquent abstractions are all very well when your
place in the world is secure and clearly defined and when financial and
moral independence are assured. It is illuminating to consider the case
of Edith Wharton, James's contemporary and friend, a novelist whose
style and subject matter have often been compared to his. Wharton, a
member of a New York aristocracy that flourished a century ago, before
it was eclipsed by New Money, had not only wealth but also taste and
a will to acquire and arrange beautiful things that was probably
unequalled in her time. She designed and furnished a series of magnificent homes for herself in the United States and Europe and wrote several books on interior design. Yet, despite being secure in her money
and having, in addition, the luxury of talent (her books had the rare fortune of being both popular and critical successes), she was nonetheless
preoccupied with the question of what it might mean to be severed
from things. In her novel *The House of Mirth* she shows her heroine inca-

pable of such separation and choosing to die rather than continue without the "shell" of wealth and social position. Lily Bart is Isabel Archer and Fleda Vetch in reverse, or put to a more extreme test than James's heroines are ever made to suffer. Stripped of things, Lily cannot survive. Or you could say that, after she takes that fatal dose of morphine at the end of the novel, she escapes into the air, Ariel-like, the place where the self resides when not anchored to the material world.

On Reading Proust

> *FOR A LONG TIME* I used to go to bed early. Sometimes, when I had put out my candle, my eyes would close so quickly that I had not even time to say to myself: "I'm falling asleep." And half an hour later the thought that it was time to go to sleep would awaken me.

*T*HE opening lines of Marcel Proust's *À la recherche du temps perdu* (*Remembrance of Things Past*, here the 1981 C. K. Scott Moncrieff and T. Kilmartin translation) contain the code of his brilliant, irritating enterprise. The first sentence refers to a generalized, repeated experience in an unsituated past time. Gradually, however, as the narrative proceeds, this unspecific and unlocalized experience of the past is anchored and particularized; it gains in texture and density. And yet this process by which the author's past life gets delineated and framed cannot be called remembering. "To remember" is to assume that something is there already to be recorded; Proust is engaged in a *"recherche,"* a "search for lost time": a scavenging into impressions and scraps of experience and an arrangement of these within an idea of the past so as to produce a literary present. Like the moment Proust records in the first lines of the novel, of waking from sleep with the thought that it is time to go to sleep, his book is the recollection of a life that is in the process of being created as he writes.

Remembrance of Things Past dazzles me because Proust is someone upon whom, as Henry James said of the great writer, "nothing is lost." It irritates me because the scavenging activity of which the book is the product is so promiscuous and obsessive that I can't help feeling put upon. Here is a narrative that seems to scorn the selectivity and order, the essential abstracting process, of narrative. I feel that Proust wants to perform an impossible acrobatic feat: to deliver himself whole onto the pages of his book—to create something in writing that is not a representation but an essence: to produce a self in and through literature that is more varied, more textured, more complete than any lived life could be.

One can look almost anywhere in Proust's mammoth work for vivid examples of this drive for totalization. All passages in the book not only contribute to the whole but are also metaphorical of the whole. For, as varied as the characters are and as confused and detailed the events and situations described, there is a sense in which everything is the same, subject to the same pattern since filtered through the same consciousness. By the same token there is almost no sense of subordination or emphasis in Proust's narrative. Its drive is above all to include and elevate everything available to that consciousness, to give everything presence and permanence.

Nonetheless, one can still have one's favorite moments in Proust, passages of special intensity that seem to contain everything that is distinctive and appealing about his style. One of these moments occurs in the third volume, entitled *Within a Budding Grove* (*À l'ombre des jeunes filles en fleurs*). The narrator, Marcel, vacationing at the seaside resort of Balbec with his grandmother and mother, encounters on the beach a group of girls who will exert an intense fascination for him. He describes his first sighting of this "little band" as follows:

> I was simply hanging about in front of the Grand Hotel until it was time for me to join my grandmother, when, still almost at the far end of the esplanade, along which they projected a striking patch of colour, I saw five or six young girls as different in appearance and manner from all the people one was accustomed to see at Balbec as would have been a flock of gulls arriving from God knows where and performing with measured tread upon the sands—the dawdlers flapping their wings to catch up with the rest—a parade the purpose of which seems as obscure to the human bathers whom they do not appear to see as it is clearly determined in their own birdish minds.
>
> One of these unknown girls was pushing a bicycle in front of her; two others carried golf-clubs; and their attire generally was in striking contrast to that of the other girls at Balbec.

The girls moving toward him are a "striking patch of color" until, seen at closer but still distant range, they remind the narrator of a flock of gulls. Then, as they continue to approach, the bird metaphor is discarded, and the girls are now perceived in terms of their equipment and attire: they are creatures of sport. Finally, when they are very close, the focus shifts yet again; the imagery now becomes artistic—pictorial (though an analogy to music is also invoked). Here is the beautiful close-up description:

> They were now quite near me. Although each was of a type absolutely different from the others, they all had beauty; but to tell the truth I had seen them for so short a time, and without venturing to look hard at them, that I had not yet individualised any of them. Except for one, whose straight nose and dark complexion singled her out from the rest, like the Arabian king in a Renaissance picture of the Epiphany, they were known to me only by a pair of hard, obstinate and mocking eyes, for instance, or by cheeks whose pinkness had a coppery tint reminiscent of geraniums; and even these features I had not yet indissolubly attached to any one of these girls rather than to another; and when (according to the order in which the group met the eye, marvellous because the most different aspects were juxtaposed, because all the colour scales were combined in it, but confused as a piece of music in which I was unable to isolate and identify at the moment of their passage the successive phrases, no sooner distinguished than forgotten) I saw a pallid oval, black eyes, green eyes, emerge, I did not know if these were the same that had already charmed me a moment ago, I could not relate them to any one girl whom I had set apart from the rest and identified. And this want, in my vision, of the demarcations which I should presently establish between them permeated the group with a sort of shimmering harmony, the continuous transmutation of a fluid, collective and mobile beauty.

Details emerge; one girl stands out for reasons of pure color and line, others blend and shift as part of the background. The narrator is at close range now and sees more and differently than at a distance, yet he continues to see a whole.

Marcel's fascination with the little band is related to the sense of abundance and variety that they offer his senses and imagination. But, whatever imagery he employs, there is always an absence of differentiating outline. At a distance his comparison is to a flock of birds, at middle range to a kind of Olympic procession, and at close range to a painting—the first, an organic phenomenon outside the laws of rational understanding; the second, a series of physical and mechical movements, a kind of coordinated machinery; the last, a spatial design, a work of art, immune to temporal ordering. If in his close-range view one girl stands out for him, "like the Arabian king in a Renaissance picture," it is not as an individual but as a point of focus, a graphic enhancement of the organicism of the whole.

The group of girls is a metaphor for Proust's literary enterprise. His goal is to render his world in all the amorphous beauty of a first impression—but working backward. For what he has to work with is not the vague impression of the moment but, instead, the particulars of experience. Indeed, Marcel's description of his first impression of the little band occurs necessarily after he has come to know them as individuals, after the group has been dispersed, both imaginatively and literally. In the course of the volume he will trace this dispersal process: his getting to know the girls, his friendship with Andrée, and his involvement with Albertine, on whom, later, he will project much of that mystical wholeness that he experienced in his first impression of the group. He will represent the folly of his attachment and the pain it will bring him. Yet though the narrative works to particularize and demythologize that original impression of a wonderfully varied, infinitely appealing whole, the larger impulse of the novel is to assemble the band of girls in all their original, undifferentiated splendor—to give the reader an image of Proust *as* the band, to produce a book that is a shimmering mass of variegated, surprising, but ultimately undifferentiatable elements.

Proust's goal in writing bears comparison with Wordsworth's—and we don't need to look only to *The Prelude*, Wordsworth's autobiographical epic poem, to make the comparison. Like Proust, Wordsworth's work has the tendency to appear both extraordinarily rich and varied and extraordinarily repetitive: each poem has its own unique life but seems to connect organically with the other poems. Any insight derived from one poem always manages to be repeated or reinforced in another— though certain poems seem more exemplary of certain points than others. Take "I Wandered Lonely as a Cloud," that deceptively simple lyric that is often read to children:

I wandered lonely as a cloud
That floats on high o'er vales and hills,
When all at once I saw a crowd,
A host, of golden daffodils;
Beside the lake, beneath the trees,
Fluttering and dancing in the breeze.

Continuous as the stars that shine
And twinkle on the milky way,
They stretched in never-ending line
Along the margin of a bay:
Ten thousand saw I at a glance,
Tossing their heads in sprightly dance.

The waves beside them danced; but they
Outdid the sparkling waves in glee;
A poet could not but be gay,
In such a jocund company;
I gazed—and gazed—but little thought
What wealth the show to me had brought:

For oft, when on my couch I lie
In vacant or in pensive mood,
They flash upon that inward eye
Which is the bliss of solitude;
And then my heart with pleasure fills,
And dances with the daffodils.

"I Wandered Lonely as a Cloud" expresses a relationship to nature and to consciousness that is representative of Wordsworth, but it is also especially well suited to the comparison I want to draw with Proust. The crowd of daffodils that surprises the poet, fluttering and dancing yet continuous, is like the band of girls. There is the same vibrancy attached to both images as well as the sense in both that the whole of that first impression is more than the sum of its parts. But, where Wordsworth recounts the original impression and tells us about how it sustains him, he also wants to differentiate the original impression from the recollection of it and the capturing of that recollection in the form of the poem. Contemplation and poetry, even when they are directed at a spontaneous undifferentiated impression, provide solace by their distance from that impression. In the shift in language from "lonely wandering" to "solitary lying," from "glee" and "gay" to "bliss" and "pleasure," the poet distinguishes between then and now, between experience and imagination, life and art. No such distinction is desired by Proust, and it is distinctions like these, in fact, that his work, neither novel nor autobiography, seem designed to obliterate.

The difference between the two writers is, I think, related to the different desires that drive them. Wordsworth is driven by the memory of childhood pleasure, Proust by childhood pain. The pleasure of childhood, though irretrievably lost to Wordsworth, exists as memory, and the mature poet seeks to use that memory as a substitute for the original pleasure. But the pain of childhood is not lost to Proust; it persists undiminished in him as an adult. Hence, it is not memory that operates, insofar as memory assumes that what is being described is gone. The experiences described are gone but not the feelings; they are as intense as ever. This is the pain that the narrator summons up so vividly in the opening pages of the book. For from the first vague reference to going to sleep ("For a long time I used to go to bed early") springs the more particular account of childhood bedtime and of the pain attached to the ritual of his mother's goodnight kiss.

Marcel describes the pleasure that this kiss brought him, but far more present to him, far more central to the ritual, was the pain associated with it. In what did that pain consist? He describes how he suffered when, owing to the presence of company, the kiss was denied him. But it is not the occasional disruption of the ritual, he gradually reveals, that was the true source of his pain. For the pain is inherent in the kiss itself—in the fact that it ends. How was he to keep his mother there and prolong that good-night kiss? No teary pleading could effect it. Even when, as he describes, his suffering became so obvious that his father, usually indifferent to his feelings, happened to notice and ordered his mother to sleep in his room, his mother's presence brought him no joy, only a more intense misery. She was now there by constraint and was disappointed in him for being "nervous." Her presence under these conditions became only another kind of loss. In short, the childhood pain of losing his mother's kiss finds no remedy in any real action; the wound only gapes further as remedies are applied. As the child grows into a man, he does not, like Wordsworth, take solace in a calm self-consciousness, a recollection in tranquillity of past feelings. Instead, he suffers that original pain with the same if not greater intensity and is thrown back to the remedies of childhood—to magical remedies now taking the form of the "magic lantern" of literature—to eternalize the ephemerality of that good-night kiss.

When I was a little girl I remember receiving a gift from an aunt who visited us. It was a little box with a transparent plastic cover, and it contained two beautifully folded cotton hankies, each with a different colored flower embroidered on it and with a little red rhinestone decorating the center of each flower. The hankies were arranged symmetrically inside the box so that the flower designs were next to each other. The delicacy of the colors on the white cloth background, the perfect crease of the linen, the springy grip of the square plastic cover on the little box—all these details are vivid in my memory. I treasured the box of hankies and never opened it. It existed for me as the very type of beauty, but that beauty consisted in my dim awareness that the hankies were meant to be used. My holding back, keeping them folded in their plastic box, was bound up with a sense that I would use them someday, that unused they were meaningless. Thus, I kept them, always intending to use them, delaying both their entry into reality and their destruction.

This is the feeling of delicious expectation that Proust describes in waiting for his mother to come up and kiss him good night, an expectation that he both wants and doesn't want fulfilled. For, if it is not fulfilled, then it entails deprivation, while, if it is, then he must be plunged into the pain of having his mother leave and the kiss be over. One way of defining art is to say that it has a self-conscious existence as a representation: it announces that, unlike my hankies or Proust's mother's kiss, it is not meant to be used and that it will not, by definition, get used up. This is the appeal of literature for Proust but also what he struggles against. He wants to preserve desire but not to acknowledge that to preserve it is to represent it and, hence, to make impossible its fulfillment. One thinks of the miser hoarding money—money that represents the power to buy things but which the miserly soul will never spend. Proust's writing is just such a hoarding of experience.

Now my five-year-old son also hoards things. After his last birth-
day he insisted on scouring the house for every gift he had received and
laying these out in front of his bed in a tightly ordered pattern. His
desire for design and order was combined, it seemed to me, with his
desire to put back, complete, make a whole—to form a bulwark and a
creative amalgam of his riches that might, when so arranged, oppose all
the disappointments that tend to accompany the pleasure of getting
presents: the fact that toys break, get lost, and are reminders of the toys
one wants but doesn't have. The first sighting of the band of girls that
Marcel describes is like my son's toys arranged in front of his bed. The
description, like everything in Proust, is an effort to control and constitute a world always on the verge of disappointment and disintegration.
In *Civilization and Its Discontents* Freud referred to what he termed the
"oceanic feeling," that momentary sense of cosmic integration that
comes to us at times and that he attributed to a vague recollection of the
womb and the mother's breast. This feeling, Freud maintained, is what
prompts people to believe in God. It also can be said to prompt a
Wordsworth or a Proust to create art, to constitute themselves as whole
and continuous through the projection onto the page of the particulars
of their experience made malleable and manipulatable through language. The difference is that Wordsworth wrote with a consciousness
that the original experience and its recovery in language were different.
In associating childhood with pleasure, Wordsworth had been "forti-
fied," to use his own word, to accept loss. For Proust, for whom childhood was associated chiefly with pain and loss, there was no such for-
tification and hence no ability to stand apart from himself and his
needs, to think about language metaphorically rather than magically.

Children do not know gratitude or moderation, perspective or
comparison. Children lack a sense of history. Proust denies history
even as he erects a literary construction that resembles a historical
record. He refuses to see his childhood pain in perspective, to allow it
to be displaced, to let it go. The drive of Proust's work is the drive to
salve childhood pain through literary expression. He hoards the particulars of the past and arranges them before his bed; he creates a magical,
invulnerable self, a literary self. Proust, like the child with his toys, is
infinitely aware and patient, but, also like the child, he lacks self-consciousness. If asked to describe the overriding tone of his great book, I
would have to say that it has the quality of a brilliant, prattling child—

one who still believes that his mother's kiss can be prolonged indefinitely, that by hoarding every nuance of what he has seen and felt he can prevent her from leaving him to face the dark alone.

"Makin' Whoopee": The Art of Female Self-Performance

*T*HERE is a movie now on videotape called *The Fabulous Baker Boys* in which brothers Beau and Jeff Bridges play brothers Frank and Jack Baker. The characters in the movie, like their real-life counterparts, also perform together, only, instead of being stars, they're dismal failures. They have a sorry little act in which they perform pop music duets on two grand pianos placed opposite each other. The concept is so depressingly bizarre that one wonders how the movie can survive it. But the movie doesn't want to sell us the act; it wants to show us what losers these brothers are. In the first half-hour of the film, we see the Baker boys slogging through their act in one seedy hotel and cocktail lounge after another, treated with contempt by slimy club managers. After fifteen years of barely surviving on the road the team has hit bottom. Frank, the older brother (played by Beau Bridges), manages the act. He's the hard-working family man with no illusions, resigned to a hand-to-mouth existence. Jack (Jeff Bridges) is the dour artistic one. When not engaged in one-night stands with cocktail waitresses, he spends his free time hanging out in a jazz club where music is presumably "taken seriously."

Once the characters and the situation are established the film assumes the task of effecting change. Responsible Frank decides they need a singer to enliven their moribund act. There follows a farcical audition scene, especially cruel in its catalog of unprepossessing female types and talent. We tolerate the heavy-handed scene because it's so clearly meant (like almost everything else in the film) as part of a setup: it prepares us for the late arrival of gum-chewingly blasé Suzie Diamond (Michelle Pfeiffer), dressed like a streetwalker (which she presumably has been until now). Of course, she is "It": the woman they and we have been waiting for. Skeptical at first, the brothers listen with increasing admiration to her slow, confident, sexy rendition of "More than You'll Know." Once she's been signed on and outfitted in more elegant though still drop-dead sexy clothes, the group begins to prosper: they play classier joints; the audiences listen and applaud; Frank is bouncy and happy; Jack seems less bitter. They begin to look like winners. And, of course, there is the requisite attraction between Jack and Suzie, which both struggle to resist in the name of professionalism.

Certainly, we've seen this kind of plot-line before—in which a group starts with nothing, makes it big, encounters problems, finds a bittersweet solution. From the moment Suzie Diamond trips outside the door of her audition, breaks her heel, yells "shit," and hobbles in looking fantastic, we know where we're heading. Why, then, does the movie work better than other versions of the same story? For it does: it made a lot of money at the box office and still does a brisk business on videotape. And I am writing about it here because, personally, I liked it a lot.

For one thing it differs from other movies in the quality of its casting. I'm not referring to the way the actors play their roles; acting in the conventional sense isn't relevant to what I mean. What seems to matter is that the actors have been matched to their roles in a way that produces in the audience an especially effective blurring of the boundaries between reality and performance. By casting the Bridges brothers as the down-and-out Baker brothers, certain physical and emotional attributes that we associate with the actors as people are brought into relief. The casting works like editorial commentary, hinting at the potential for decline lurking in the careers of Beau and Jeff Bridges and teasing us with the possibilities of what they may "really" feel about each other. The casting of Michelle Pfeiffer as the charismatic singer with the slatternly past also speaks to our sense of the actress as a real person—to the dissonance that exists between Pfeiffer's too-pretty face and the accomplished performer she has shown herself to be. There is even a pleasing doppelgänger quality to the names Michelle Pfeiffer and Suzie Diamond: the fictional name seems to parody the actress's "real" name, flattening and vulgarizing what, by contrast, seems artificially elegant and ethereal. It's generally unheard of to use actors for something more than their reputations as actors, to start fiddling with the baggage that surrounds them as people—but the fact is that that baggage is always there, operating on us in some way. A film like this, which actually seems to capitalize upon this baggage in a consistent way, has a new kind of power over its audience. It is as though the actors are not pretending to be someone else but are acting at being themselves in some stylized, Kabuki-like way.

But the movie also uses this blurring of reality and performance in a way that reaches beyond the individual actors to a more general statement about performance itself, specifically female performance. The performance of Michelle Pfieffer as Suzie Diamond is at the center of the film; it saves the film quite as much as it saves the brothers' act inside the film. What is there about this performance that is so appealing, that speaks so eloquently to its audience of mostly women (for it was women who went to see this movie in droves)?

What the film enacts is a female fantasy of self-performance. Although Suzie Diamond is made responsible for saving the group and bringing them success, it is not her voice that is focused on. The casting of Michelle Pfeiffer, not known to be singer, immediately identifies the singing as something of secondary importance in the film's system of values. It is not her voice but her *self* that the movie cares about. It is Suzie Diamond's self-performance that the movie celebrates. Her singing simply offers a particularly expressive vehicle for her to shine as a richly textured and impressive character, as a seductive personality, and as someone whom Jack and the audience must fall in love with.

The fantasy of self-performance is most completely brought home to us in one scene toward the middle of the film. The scene takes place on New Year's Eve and has Suzie draped over Jack's piano singing the song "Makin' Whoopee" to an appreciative audience. With the arrival of this scene we are suddenly made aware of how necessary are the plot details that came before. Fantasy depends upon narrative buildup for its link to reality, for the sense that it is emerging naturally out of circumstances and events as they might happen. Hence, in fantasizing, we artificially erect the situation out of which the fantasy is then made naturally to spring. The movie imitates this process, and we accept the cumbersome quality of the plot and the contrived (even boring) interactions that set up the characters and events, in order to achieve the payoff in this one perfectly orchestrated scene. Thus, it happens that, on this particular night, the older brother has been called home to deal with a family emergency. For once, then, the Jeff Bridges character and the Michelle Pfeiffer character are left to perform together. This removal of the third works dramatically, since the presence of the responsible, married older brother has, until now, blocked the romantic intimacy between the other two characters, although this blockage has also served to heighten the sexual tension between them. And, indeed, to block or delay the enactment of a fantasy is part of preparing for it: it helps give the fantasy its extemporaneous quality.

We can also see, once we arrive at this scene, how effective the seemingly unwieldy idea of the musical duo is to the fantasy element in the film. The brothers begin as a failing team, add a singer, and begin to have success; as this occurs, a new dyad begins to take shape within the triad, fueled by the romantic attraction between Jack and Suzie. This covert dyad is built on the drama implicit in the female performing to the admiring, if resistant, gaze of the male. Up until the New Year's Eve performance Jack has been able to resist Suzie because of the buffer of his brother. Now that Frank is absent, he is exposed. At the same time, this places a special kind of pressure on the woman. She has her chance to seduce the man, but she also knows that the opportunity is short-lived and fragile; she must rise to the occasion, rally all her resources, be the best she can be. And the movie, as fantasy, operates to support her.

Everything happens just as it should. It is New Year's Eve; the characters are alone at a fancy resort hotel; she is exquisitely dressed; and the song that she is to perform is the right one. Standing on top of the piano she begins the most commanding, the most slithery, the most broad and amusing and seductive rendition of "Makin' Whoopee" one could possibly imagine. It is a tour de force of performance, not only because it is interpretively compelling but also because it uses every-thing that the character has: her looks, her clothes (scanty as they are), her long legs (which, to dramatize the final lines of the song, step con-fidently down from the top of the piano onto the keyboard to the ground), her hair, her voice, her sense of humor, her intelligence. It is a creative expression and an assertion of power—power over the absolutely enrapt Jack, who is accompanying her performance as if in a dream, over the drunken hotel audience, who grow hushed and atten-tive as she sings, and, if I extrapolate from my own reaction, over the movie audience, who cannot help but succumb to the spell. It is a moment that can't last, but while it does, it is perfect. It is a fantasy in which the female seduces the male, but, in orchestrating her perfor-mance so perfectly, she also transcends the discreet goal of seduction: she controls the world through the artful presentation of herself. She achieves temporary omnipotence. Everything from here on out is and must be downhill. But that's okay. One accepts the perfunctory promise of the ending, knowing that there just is no way that the movie could top that performance of "Whoopee"—that beautifully choreographed performance of self.

Self-performance as a female fantasy has been written about before. After I watched the movie I remembered an essay on "Performing Heroines" by Ellen Moers in her 1977 book *Literary Women*. She describes the same effect produced on her by the heroine of the nineteenth-century novel by Madame de Staël, *Corinne*. De Staël's novel resembles *The Fabulous Baker Boys* in some striking ways, if you correct for differences in the media involved and for contextual differences that have to do with the democratizing of the feminine ideal since de Staël's time. Corinne is a young woman of noble birth who lives alone in Rome, where she has attained an extraordinary reputation for beauty and style and for her talents as poet, translater, dancer, and improviser. The high point of the novel occurs when she is made the toast of Rome in a kind of coronation scene. Corinne parades through the city, applauded by multitudes, while her English admirer, Oswald, looks on. She is dressed exquisitiely in white robes (Pfeiffer's red minidress is an opposite but comparably emphatic garb in her scene), and her grace and nobility are dazzling to the throng of onlookers, to Oswald, and to the reader. When Corinne reaches the Capitol she mounts the steps and delivers a brilliant extemporaneous speech, enthralling the citizens of Rome much as Michelle Pfeiffer as Suzie Diamond enthralls her rowdy New Year's Eve audience. The notion of improvisation is important to the novel, as it is to the movie, for it implies that the heroine is expressing her inherent qualities through the medium of her art—that what is impressive is not so much her expertise as a performer as her rendering of her natural self through the artifice of performance.

Moers goes on to explain that Corinne is de Staël's own personal fantasy, a fantasy that she went far to realize in her lifetime. During the nineteenth century de Staël was a star, adulated not only in France but throughout Europe as a woman of genius. She was, claims Moers, a celebrity equal in stature to Napoléon, only her empire was the feminine domain of the salon.

But, in rereading Moers's discussion of de Staël, what struck me now most of all was Moers's own delightful, imperial style. I realized that she was participating in the fantasy she described and that *Literary*

Women is, above all, a self-performance—a brilliant improvisation. Moers interprets, or "performs," the character of de Staël and other neglected female writers with humor, insight, and virtuosity, and she takes them over, and us, too, in the process.

Interestingly, however, Moers ends by criticizing the self-performance of de Staël and of her fictional alter ego, Corinne. Although she acknowledges their appeal, she denigrates the impulses that drive them as antithetical to the kind of work that's worth doing. She laments the dispersion of energy that self-performance requires of women, causing them to focus on self-projection rather than self-mastery, and she is unsympathetic to female characters, whether real or fictional, who seem to have succumbed to the myth of Corinne. Dorothea Brooke, in *Middlemarch*, is, according to Moers, one unfortunate result of such influence: "she is good for nothing *but* to be admired . . . an arrogant, selfish, spoiled, rich beauty, she does little but harm in the novel." Sylvia Plath is another, she says—a contemporary, real-life victim of self-performance, a woman so consumed with the need to embody an image of talent and sensitivity that she could not do her work, could not even keep herself alive. More than the lack of a room of their own, Moers concludes, the training of women in performance may be the source of their failure to write.

Implicit in Moers's argument is her sense that only writing is real accomplishment and that, driven by a fantasy that seeks to move from the page onto the stage of life, women get into trouble and squander their literary gifts. Her argument seems grounded in the assumptions of the feminist movement of her time, the early 1970s, when women were just beginning to find their voices as critics and were making some perceptible headway in academia. But today, after numerous setbacks and defeats for feminism and after the movement itself has begun to question many of its goals and premises, Moers's ideas about how women ought to direct their energy seem overly narrow and naive. Isn't the drive for bottom-line accomplishment, which Moers argues for, another and perhaps more insidious form of self-performance, of women doing what they feel contemporary society now expects of them? By the same token, in elevating the myth of female writing as a means of self-fulfillment and denigrating a more diffuse kind of expression, I wonder whether Moers isn't buying into a traditional male value system quite as much as those she condemns. Why must concrete accomplishment be the goal of a woman's life? More-over, for all that performance for women may be the result of patriar-chal dictates and expectations, is it not possible to see the fantasy as potentially empowering, reaching beyond the principles that informed it and transforming them in the process? Can a drive to appear pleasing in the eyes of men ultimately lead beyond that ostensible object—lead, that is, to the creation of an independent, powerful, and creative per-sonality?

It may be because of an intuition of such an outcome that Ameri-can society has traditionally placed limits on female self-performance even as it has encouraged it. The Miss America contest, that quintes-sentially American exhibition of a female ideal, is about drawing these kind of limits: it enumerates what ought to constitute proper self-per-formance and how much weight the qualities involved should carry. In the society of the 1950s, in which a conventional image of femininity held sway, women accepted the notion that physical appearance and manners were primary and that intelligence and talent were secondary or even of negative value. With the women's movement, however, the number of qualities deemed acceptable for women to possess expanded. Hence, any explicit system of judgment now appears to limit and trivialize female self-performance; the beauty contest now seems anachronistic less for what it contains than for what it fails to include. The premise behind the contest still operates, only now the runway has become the larger runway of life.

The appeal of the "Whoopee" scene in *The Fabulous Baker Boys* lies in the way it plays with old and new ideas of self-performance, blurring the boundaries in much the same way that it blurs the boundaries between the real lives of its performers and the characters they play. The climac-tic scene in which Suzie Diamond performs on New Year's Eve resem-bles the old-fashioned beauty pageant, in that it involves a circum-scribed space and capitalizes on physical exhibitionism; the piano is, literally, a runway on which the female character parades herself. Looks and charm and feminine seductiveness are very much part of the effectiveness of this performance. But the character Suzie Diamond, as played by Michelle Pfeiffer, is also a working singer, and in life an accomplished actress. The character is portrayed as tough and autonomous, and she brings to her physical self-display a good deal of wit and shrewd calculation. While the act seems spontaneous, it is clearly the work of a pro, someone who knows how to make things look effortless. Suzie Diamond is a pro with men as well; for all that her relationship with the leading man seems to take forever to get off the ground, in the end, after trying a whole range of strategies, she wins him, and not just for her bed—she converts him from one-night stands to commitment, and, more impressive still, she makes him talk. She gets him on her own terms, choreographing her world as she choreographs her rendering of that song and the response it elicits. Here is a woman performing herself *as a woman,* precariously close to caricature (there is a large dose of self-mockery in that rendition of "Makin' Whoopee"), who nonetheless manages to steal the show. In short, she enacts the female stereotype and transcends it by working so expertly within the genre of self-performance.

Love and Pity

"*S*HE loved me for the dangers I had passed," explains Othello of his love for Desdemona, "And I loved her that she did pity them." These lines have always struck me as significant, and I am convinced that Shakespeare had in mind a glimpse into the destructive way that gender roles shape romantic love in Western culture when he assigned them to Othello early in the play.

A close study of the lines shows them not to be as clear and straightforward as they might at first appear to be. An odd suggestion of sequence (first she loved me, then I loved her), a layering of causality (she loved me for one thing, I loved her for another, but related, thing), and a slippage in pronoun reference ("she did pity them" rather than the more logical "she did pity me") create an evocative, overdetermined effect. If one begins to tease out meanings from these lines, one finds that they code the multiple, sometimes contradictory impulses that fuel cases of domestic violence.

In the first line Othello ascribes to Desdemona the initiating role in the affair—she succumbed, it seems, to a simple case of hero worship: she loved him for his bravery and fortitude in the face of dangers. The second line, however, shifts to proclaim his own love for her as the result of another response that he ascribes to her—her pity. But pity for what? The pronoun is unexpected: not "And I loved her that she did pity me" but "And I loved her that she did pity them." Pitying the dangers makes no sense unless one is to assume that she pitied any adversary who would dare confront the powerful Othello, a foreshadowing perhaps of her own eventual status as his victim (she will indeed be pitiable). But this idea, though prophetic, simply doesn't fit the mood of the line. Clearly, Othello has in mind her pity for him as one who has suffered in the face of dangers. The faulty use of the pronoun *them* (when *me* would scan as well) suggests that he needs to deflect her pity for him rhetorically, even as he acknowledges it as the source of his love for her.

In Othello's linking of love and pity—and his veering away from that link at the same time—Shakespeare was anatomizing the psychology of Othello and Desdemona's relationship and anticipating problems. Pity is an expression of compassion, but of compassion tinged with condescension. Othello's ascribing pity to Desdemona suggests that he feels inferior; her professed love is for his heroism, but his own view of himself leads him to trust more to her pity than to her love as security for their union. In the play he is her social inferior; her father is at first furious at her marriage to a Moor. By the same token Desdemona's pity for Othello can be understood as her perhaps unconscious effort first to put him in his place, then to blunt the edge of her hero worship so that it will not be as consuming. He is a great warrior, she only a weak and helpless female; her pity elevates her to the position of the great lady, even though in reality she is no more than chattel in her father's house and will occupy a similar position in her husband's.

If pity is understood as a means of humanizing but also humbling its object, one can understand why female pity might be at the root of male violence: it feeds male insecurity and, instead of doing what Virginia Woolf has explained is the traditional function of the woman in a relationship, "reflecting the figure of a man at twice his natural size," ties her love to his diminishment. Perhaps Othello's fury at being told about Desdemona's infidelity springs from this source: it was not that she loved someone else but, rather, that she was laughing at him with someone else—that her pity had turned to contempt. Cassio, Othello's supposed rival, in being more conventional and "mainstream" in appearance and manners, makes him just the figure likely to be complicit in Desdemona's ridicule. Othello's belief in an alliance between Desdemona and Cassio demonstrates how fragile his initial security in his wife's love really was. It suggests that her admiration for the obstacles he has had to surmount can easily change into distaste for his being who he was to begin with: an outsider. One could imagine this scenario as operating in the case of O. J. Simpson, a celebrity football hero with roots in the ghetto who chose to marry a sexy blond—the society's symbol of the ultimate sexual trophy. How much did his sense of being an outsider propel him into that marriage (playing to her admiration for his heroic rise) and then drive him to abuse and possibly murder as he saw himself reduced back to being the outsider again?

Yet there is clearly some sense in which Othello sought Desdemona's pity. It is her pity for him, after all, that he cites not as the catalyst for her love for him but, instead, as the catalyst for his love for her. This suggests that he desires pity, though he may, at the same time, deny or resent being pitied. This need for pity seems to spring from the enormous pressures that being a man places on him. Consider the full passage in which he describes Desdemona's falling in love:

> Her father loved me; oft invited me;
> Still questioned me the story of my life
> From year to year, the battle, sieges, fortune
> That I have passed.
> I ran it through, even from my boyish days
> To th'very moment that he bade me tell it.
> Wherein I spoke of most disastrous chances,
> Of moving accidents by flood and field,
> Of hairbreadth scapes i' th' imminent deadly breach,
> Of being taken by the insolent foe
> And sold to slavery, of my redemption thence
> And portance in my travel's history,
> Wherein of anters vast and deserts idle,
> Rough quarries, rocks, and hills whose heads touch heaven,
> It was my hint to speak. Such was my process.

Othello presents himself here as doing Desdemona's father's bidding and earning his love by reciting his exploits. He is the man's man on parade—giving precisely the tales of heroism and toughness that the father wants to bolster his own masculine self-image. That Othello is also a Moor, an outsider to the white, aristocratic society embodied by Desdemona's father, only makes his need to prove himself and be loved that much greater. It also explains the quality of subservience in the performance, the sense we have that he is reciting his exploits on command, perhaps embroidering them to live up to some preconceived notion of the prowess and heroism of the exotic warrior.

It happens, however, that Desdemona is also the audience to these tales. She, as Othello puts it, would

> . . . come again, and with a greedy ear
> Devour up my discourse. Which I observing,
> Took once a pliant hour, and found good means

> To draw from her a prayer of earnest heart
> That I would all my pilgrimage dilate.

Just as he has been the "pliant" entertainer of the father, he now becomes such an entertainer to the daughter. Othello is convinced that Desdemona craves hearing his exploits, that they excite her: "often did [I] beguile her of her tears / When I did speak of some distressful stroke / That my youth suffered." Here, presumably, is where the pity comes into play, but, as Othello tells it, Desdemona is more like the audience to a gladiatorial encounter than a compassionate soul mate. She is responding to an exaggerated idea of masculine prowess that he accommodatingly provides for her. Indeed, he is operating in the same way as he makes his case about the validity of his marriage, reciting the same kinds of exploits that evoked the reaction from Desdemona (and, before her, from her father). As with her, moreover, he is able once again to win over his audience: the Duke is moved to admiration, and the father relents.

Yet there is an unconscious gap in Othello's expression of what arouses love and what he actually needs: "She loved me for the dangers I had passed, / And I loved her that she did pity them." In telling his tales to Desdemona, Othello clearly had in mind a different kind of recital than the one he offered to her father. He doesn't seek to give the listener reinforcement in a male role; he wants, rather, to delineate dif-ference—to show Desdemona the perils attached to being a man as opposed to a woman, to arouse her pity. Othello's words suggest that women love men for being heroic but that men want women to feel the toll that heroism takes on them. This reading puts an entirely different spin on what may have precipitated Othello's violence. He loves Des-demona because he thinks she pities him, but perhaps it is that she doesn't that lies at the root of the problem. She accompanies him on his campaign because, in her words, "I saw Othello's visage in his mind,/And to his honors and his valiant parts/Did I my soul and for-tunes consecrate." Pity seems to have been left behind here. She has consecrated herself to the warrior, the hero, the male paragon, and it is to a notion of male honor, a derivative of these very things, that she is eventually sacrificed.

The two responses to pity that I have outlined as contained in Oth-ello's situation—resentment of pity for making him feel diminished and desire for pity as providing an opening for weakness and simple humanity—define the parameters within which domestic violence happens. And it seems clear that, ultimately, the two are not distinct but interconnected responses. It is precisely in a climate in which men are not supposed to be pitiful that pity, when it is introduced, can wield a devastating blow to self-esteem.

Alfred Hitchcock's 1958 film *Vertigo* has certain interesting affinities with *Othello*. Indeed, the film seems to me to extend the implications of the Shakespearean tragedy into a contemporary arena and to give the characteristics associated with Othello a more explicit "everyman" representation. That *Vertigo* was made during a period in which sex roles were strictly defined in American culture makes it all the more interesting, for it can be read as a commentary on the transition from 1950s conventionality to the social rebelliousness and gender questioning of the 1960s and 1970s.

James Stewart, who plays the protagonist, Scottie Ferguson, is not an outsider by birth in the way Othello is, but he becomes one. He "falls" literally into that position when he fails to perform his work as a detective (losing his footing during a rooftop chase) and becomes riddled with fear (which manifests itself as the condensed symptom of vertigo). The film follows his attempt to rebuild himself as a masculine prototype (the tough detective he once was) as he agrees to do some sleuthing for an old friend who is concerned about the safety of his wife. The wife, Madeleine Elster (Kim Novak), is a beautiful, mysterious woman who looks to him for support (without making demands or showing any interest in his past). With her admiring, helpless gaze upon him (like Desdemona's tearful gaze on Othello as he recited his exploits), Scottie bolsters his sense of self; he falls in love and seems to regain confidence. But suddenly Madeleine kills herself and in such a way that he appears partially responsible. Her death shatters the fragile structure of his identity once again. When he finally recovers from this second mental breakdown, he makes one last effort toward rehabilitating his old self: he finds and reshapes another woman into the image of the lost Madeleine. But the trauma is not yet complete. He will eventually discover that the two women are the same person: that the so-called Madeleine had been hired to serve as the cover for another woman's murder and had then allowed Scottie to make her over into the image of what she had previously pretended to be. Scottie reacts explosively to this knowledge, this time precipitating the real death of the woman he had loved.

At the center of this film is the pitiable aspect of the male protagonist, unwilling to accept pity but unable to maintain the artificial strength associated with the masculine role. He is left, in the end, staring down into an abyss in which he has lost both women, really the same woman—or, rather, the idea of Woman as a prop for his masculinity. On the margins of the film has existed all along the pedestrian Midge, whose love is explicitly linked to pity and, since it feeds rather than counters his sense of male insufficiency, cannot be reciprocated.

Both Shakespeare and Hitchcock were delineating a basic lack in their male protagonists, a failure of self-examination that seems linked to the heroic notion of masculinity. If Othello knows enough to know he needs pity, which is more than Scottie can admit, he still is unable to deal with being pitied, or imagining that he is, on a day-to-day basis. In both cases the inability of the male character to deal with the possibility of his own weakness involves the projection onto the woman of that weakness. This results in the abuse of the woman, who must pay when the man feels he has not lived up to the ideal he has created (or, rather, that his society has thrust upon him).

Yet there is a secondary effect to this projection of weakness onto the woman as it serves to bolster the protagonist's masculine ego. It carries with it other projections relating to all that which cannot be encompassed within the simple container of the masculine ideal. Hence, in *Vertigo* Madeleine emerges not just as an embodiment of weakness and vulnerability but also as the repository of all that is unassimilable within the recipe of heroic action. In short, she serves as the prosthetic unconscious for Scottie, the place where his moral complexity and emotional depth can be stored—which explains why her loss is so utterly devastating to him. Film theorists who argue that the woman exists in classical narrative fim as a simple fetish object for the male spectator seem to miss the more evocative qualities associated with the female representation. For, while the woman may exist thematically as an object and victim of male power, she also inhabits the role of a subjectivity and is often more imaginatively compelling and potentially transformative than her male counterpart. Here, then, is another take on what happens in cases of domestic violence: the male turns on the woman both because she makes him feel less confident in his masculine role *and* because she embodies an idea of subjectivity that is more complex, multifaceted, and open to difference than he is permitted. He seeks to crush that subjectivity out of jealousy; he wants but doesn't dare to have it for himself. In such a reading the green-eyed monster that inhabits Othello would be directed not at some imagined rival but at the woman herself, whose presence at the site of battle becomes a reminder that heroic deeds may not be worth pursuing—that he'd rather have the luxury of thought and feeling.

As a coda, let me add that I have always felt torn between admiration and pity for men (a set of contradictory sentiments that I would abbreviate as the Desdemona complex). I can trace these feelings back to childhood feelings about my father, whom I deeply admired but whom I also learned to pity, largely through cues from my mother, who, when she was not furious with him, tended to take a pitying tone in discussing him. This was her method, I sensed, of registering her superiority (despite his ostensibly greater clout in the family) but also of acknowledging the difficulties attached to his role. From my mother I intuited the idea that women, though they might have fewer concrete opportunities in life, were less burdened by the truly onerous and dangerous kinds of social expectations that men faced. This left women psychologically freer and made them more grown-up than men. I learned to connect my father's bursts of temper (my mother called them his "tantrums") with some vague, inexplicit pressure that he was continually under and that he could not admit; hence, he lashed out at us. In our household we had to be careful not to express our pity of him too directly—this infuriated him: he interpreted it as condescension (which in some sense it was), and he would not be condescended to. Yet his tantrums were as often about our supposed neglect of his "feelings," as he called them. I have since interpreted this as his way of demanding that we acknowledge the strain he was under as a man—in short, that we pity him.

The dynamic of love and pity that was set in motion during my childhood has continued in my dealings with men as I have grown older. Thus, my tolerance for boorishness and self-aggrandizement among men is very great; I rationalize this behavior by imagining that beneath lies a kinder and gentler soul that cannot find a proper means of expressing itself. This makes me a good listener, one in whom men can confide, but in a number of cases it has led to scenes in which the men in question, sensing my pity, have sought to reduce me to tears. They want to erase the sensation of being pitied by occupying the role of tyrant. Men who have been brutish or nasty until I cry then become conciliatory: they have achieved their goal. Ironically, however, these episodes only reinforce my conviction that they are truly pitiable, that they are, in fact, the emotionally deprived individuals that I suspected they were. This power dynamic operates, I suspect, in more extreme cases of abuse in which both partners seek reinforcement for their own position—and get it in the culminating act of violence. Unfortunately for women, the reinforcement they gain must be paid for in physical suffering—a high price to pay for being right. But, then, men have been expected to die on battlefields in accordance to the dictates of heroic masculinity, so perhaps the exchange has not been so unequal. In other words, it seems important to recognize the way in which gender conventions compose a far-reaching system of social responses such that blame cannot be easily isolated in one sex.

This recognition has been reinforced in me since I had a son. We live in a fairly typical suburban community in which success at team sports is a defining factor in a boy's life. Masculinity is computed by the ability to make hits, throw far and accurately, not cry when hurt during play, and aggressively pursue the ball (even if it means plowing into an opponent). Recently, I stood with a group of mothers at a soccer game and watched them scream at their boys: "Show some hustle," "Be aggressive," "Act like a man"—their faces contorted with competitive fervor. Perhaps it was their own desire to be out there that had been sublimated into this ferocious cheerleading; perhaps it was the conviction that they must condition their sons into a conventional masculinity if they were to survive the trials of growing up. Whatever the reason, their focus on the nine-year-olds in the field was intense and gladiatorial, and I felt myself caught up in the gladiatorial spirit, just as eager for my son to kick and shove his way to victory as they were for theirs. And acknowledging that I felt this made me sad. We mothers, whom one might have thought would be the ultimate refuges for weakness, were, at that moment, conditioning our sons into a form of aggressive behavior that they could not possibly sustain beyond the playing field for very long and yet one that we were signaling was to be the emblem of their masculinity. Later we would offer them solace, but it would be too late, for it would now be something that we had schooled them to resent. The image of masculinity that the playing field teaches and that we buy into as rooting mothers does not admit weakness. Hence, the simple love that as mothers we might give must now be transmuted into pity—pity that our boys desire but can't accept. Like Desdemona, it would seem that we must be held at least partially responsible for any violence our sons might one day commit in their desire for and resentment of such pity.

I do believe, as my mother taught me, that women have far more freedom to deviate from a standard of gender behavior than men. But that freedom is irrelevant and may even be an incitement to abuse, since women's lives are so enmeshed with the lives of men. Based on my own response at the soccer game, a masculine standard of behavior is deeply entrenched even and perhaps especially in the soft hearts of mothers—and it is mothers, sisters, daughters, and wives who will have to pay when men find themselves falling short of that standard. The following anecdote speaks to the issue. It is said to have occurred between the frontier leader Andrew Jackson, when he was a boy, and his mother:

> "Stop that, Andrew. Do not let me see you cry again. Girls were made to cry, not boys."
> "What are boys made for, mother?"
> "To fight."

There, it seems, are the roots of a great warrior. When he falls short of the heroic ideal his mother taught him (as he inevitably must), he will find solace not in his own tears but in making women cry.

The Birth and Death of the Unconscious

*T*WO conversations I had recently started me thinking about the way meaning has evolved and is evolving in our culture. One of these conversations was with my sister, the other with a close female friend. Both women had just discovered they were pregnant. With my sister I had been discussing our work—we are both writers—and she had been complaining to me about the difficulty she was having getting a manuscript placed. I thought it might help to put things in perspective.

"Think," I said, "of how insignificant this is in comparison to the way you felt about having a baby. How you promised yourself that if only you could get pregnant you wouldn't care about these sorts of things as much anymore."

"What are you talking about?" she said with surprise. "I never made that kind of promise to myself."

"But you were so worried about not being able to get pregnant," I reminded her.

"Well, I wanted to have a baby, but it wasn't an obsession," she countered with a certain annoyance. "I didn't feel I was trading all my other concerns for it."

A few days later, a conversation with my friend took a similar turn. I had been congratulating her on the news of her pregnancy.

"And to think you were once so adamant about not having children," I said.

"Adamant?" she seemed surprised. "I was never adamant about not having children."

"But I remember you said you didn't want children."

"I may have said that at one time," she shrugged irritably. "The whole idea didn't interest me then, but I was never adamant. I just knew I wasn't ready. And now I am."

These conversations might suggest that I was a poor listener and distorted what my sister and my friend said. This may be true, but, if so, I want to ignore this supposed truth and discover why I listened poorly and distorted the messages I received. I want to argue that my particular relationship to meaning in both of these cases is grounded in ideas conditioned into us all since the nineteenth century. As modern selves, we have learned to expect others to disguise unconsciously some part of what they feel. If the original words spoken by my sister and my friend were not as explicit or emphatic as I understood them to be, I put this down to their unconscious dissimulation of what they felt at the time. And certainly I am not prompted to give up my initial interpretations of their past reactions based on their current disclaimers but, rather, to use the disclaimers as reinforcement for my original interpretations. These women, I conclude, are unconscious of the degree to which they felt what they felt; they have repressed memories of their desires and fears. The peevishness with which they respond to my questioning only convinces me further that I am right.

Freud paved the way for this kind of reasoning about a century ago in his "Fragment of an Analysis of a Case of Hysteria," more popularly known as the "Dora case." The case contains an extremely straightforward assertion of one of the most central and revolutionary principles of Freud's method. "If "the 'No' uttered by a patient after a repressed thought has been presented to his conscious perception for the first time . . . is ignored," explains Freud in his introductory remarks, "evidence soon begins to appear that in such a case 'No' signifies the desired 'Yes.'" This statement becomes the basis for his interpretation of the precipitating event of Dora's symptoms: her rejection of the amorous advances of her father's friend Herr K. (the man who happens to be the husband of her father's lover, a woman to whom Dora had been closely attached). Dora's rejection of Herr K. is interpreted by Freud to mean its opposite: it stands for her *unconscious* attraction to Herr K., an attraction that, Freud goes on to postulate, substitutes in its turn for Dora's still more deeply unconscious incestuous love for her father and her homosexual attraction to Frau K.

This complicated line of reasoning may seem fantastic in summary, but, as Freud develops it, it becomes persuasive. As he traces connections and "excavates" buried meaning (the archaeological metaphor is employed extensively), what draws us on is less the actual argument than the general method. Freud's rule about disclaimers is emblematic of this method because it so dramatically demonstrates his capacity to salvage meaning from what on the surface looks intractible. Indeed, the more seemingly intractible the surface statement, the better suited it appears to be to Freud's interpretive method. Although Dora breaks off the analysis before it is completed, thereby appearing to invalidate her case for study, Freud employs the "No-signifies-Yes" dictum to turn her breaking with him into a highly signficant act, one that really expresses her dependence—that signals, in other words, the intensity of her transference onto him of those very desires that weave their way back through Herr K. to her father and to Frau K. While Freud admits that he was clumsy in allowing things to get to the point of actual rupture, he is nonetheless able to use the rupture to extraordinarily fruitful interpretive ends. It becomes, if anything, the concrete "proof" of his theory about Dora, since it repeats the pattern of negation that he has traced in the analysis.

Freud did not initiate this creative attitude toward meaning; he only gave it systematic form. The whole of late-nineteenth-century European culture evolved to produce a climate in which such ideas might flourish. One thinks of George Eliot, for example, whose novels concern themselves almost exclusively with conscious motive and with the importance of the human will—very different concerns from Freud's. Yet consider the implications of an extemporaneous discourse that one contemporary observer records her delivering. The subject, as reported, was "God, Immortality, and Duty." "How inconceivable was the *first*," she is said to have maintained, "how unbelievable the *second*, and yet how peremptory and absolute the *third*." Eliot pronounced here what would become an increasingly commonplace assumption in Victorian culture: that we must act dutifully even as we admit that there is no longer a compelling outside convention, neither God nor Immortality, to supply meaning. But it follows from this extremity that we would then seek to supply meaning through some alternative, personally devised means. It is for this reason that Eliot's greatest protagonists, when they act dutifully, take on a sharper, more distinctive identity. In *Middlemarch* the more Dorothea Brooke abases herself to her awful husband, the more odd and interesting she becomes—and, indeed, though the novel doesn't state this, one can't help feeling that what attracts the young Ladislaw to Dorothea is precisely her extraordinarily dutiful behavior toward his abhorred uncle. Dorothea's exaggerated sense of duty is suggestive of any number of hidden things, and to say that it suggests masochistic desire is only one especially crude example of those things.

The effort to fill the hollow forms of daily life with personal meaning becomes the central preoccupation of Henry James, who, like Freud, was still relatively young when Eliot spoke those portentous words late in her career. Although James's early heroine, Isabel Archer, is a fairly conventional portrait of what may result when one is thrown upon one's own resources to determine meaning and value, his later heroines move far beyond Isabel in the extent of their creative, interpretive powers. In *The Golden Bowl* the heroine, Maggie Verver, marries someone who (like Gilbert Osmond, Isabel's nemesis of a husband in *Portrait of a Lady*) seems the embodiment of conventional loyalties and standards, tradition-bound and inflexible. In this novel, however, the heroine's ability to bring her creative vision to bear on her situation makes it possible for her to sustain a belief in her husband's "personal sovereignty" even in the face of his horrendous behavior—that is, to eclipse convention with imagination, or, more correctly, to bring into question the whole notion of what consitutes fact and fiction. The power of creative interpretation reigns supreme in this novel, and it appears at once a saving perspective and a frightening one in its ability to make everything bend before it.

There is a correspondence to be drawn between James's American girl heroine in *The Golden Bowl* and the Viennese Jew who became the father of psychoanalysis—the idea of transference is the bridge between them. Maggie's efforts in the novel are directed toward restoring her relationship with her adulterous husband (a restoration that is, in fact, a creation, since that relationship is not so much rebuilt as forged on a deeper level). This task is performed, however, through the *opposite* of conventional means. As Dorothea Krook explained in her classic study of James, the heroine moves toward her goal "precisely by not insisting: by not pressing or harassing her husband the Prince but instead, simply letting him alone." Freud based his therapeutic method on a similar strategy of self-effacement. The patient, he believed, should work through childhood trauma by projecting onto the therapist the emotions felt toward the parents. The therapist, therefore, was expected to exist as a screen, opaque and available for projection. But both James's heroine and Freud are not just screens; they exist in positions of creative power in relation to their subjects because they possess

a theory of meaning as more than surface expression. This theory, even when left unarticulated, directs others in the way meaning should be approached. By withdrawing her influence from her husband but not explaining that withdrawal, Maggie initiates a new kind of secretiveness, different from the old-style secretiveness of adultery, which her husband and stepmother have been engaged in. What is secret is knowledge, not action. Maggie's husband does not know what she knows, and, as a result, her value becomes heightened for him, her character deepens in his eyes: "Your husband has never, never, never—
. . . Never been half so interested in you as now," Maggie's friend tells her as her strategy begins to take effect. And, as the Prince's interest in his wife grows, his own character seems to thicken: his motives appear to multiply and grow more complicated. In the Prince, James shows us the birth of the unconscious as linked to an awakening sense of the enigmatic quality of the Other. Likewise, it is precisely Freud's presence beside his patients, silently listening, that interposes between him and them the sense of a meaning beyond that which they think they know. From the sense of that mysterious Other, the patients are then spurred to the imagination of a deeper, more mysterious self.

In short, the need to see the Other as mysterious arose in a world grown bereft of other sources of meaning and value. And a view of the Other as deep and strange doubled back to affect the view of oneself. This is precisely what happens, according to Freud, in the formation of the unconscious: "we call a psychical process unconscious whose existence we are obliged to assume—for some such reason as that we infer it from its effects—, but of which we know nothing. In that case we have the same relation to it as we have to a psychical process in another person, except that it is in fact one of our own." Freud then goes on at some length to explain the relationship between the conscious and the unconsious—that is, the notion of self as that which is available to us and of self as that which is foreign. The assertion of a connecting relationship between these two processes or parts of the self is necessary, since to make ourselves totally inaccessible to ourselves would preclude the possibility of interpreting ourselves. We must, it seems, have just enough awareness to make what we do not know a subject of endless fascination and speculation.

The discovery of the unconscious is the initiation, therefore, of an activity as well as of a concept, reinforcing my earlier point that it fills a cultural vacuum once filled by religion. By ferreting out the meanings of others and of ourselves we not only infuse meaning into the world but also give ourselves something to do. We engage in a quest that has no ostensible end, that seeks nothing more than the pleasure of knowledge while continually deferring the satisfaction of complete understanding. In his late essay "Analysis Terminable and Interminable," Freud makes it clear that the practical issue of terminating an analysis is quite another thing from the analytical mode of thought, which must be carried on in perpetuity: "we reckon on the stimuli that he has received in his own analysis not ceasing when it ends and on the processes of remodelling the ego continuing spontaneously in the analysed subject and making use of all subsequent experiences in this newly-acquired sense." At the foundation of this process, Freud notes, there must be "a firm conviction of the existence of the unconscious."

This ongoing analytical relationship to experience has now, it seems, become a prominent element in our culture. It fuels tabloid journalism and talk shows, and it has, in fact, become the mechanism according to which all reporting is carried out. Beginning with the assumption that something is hidden, the reporter relentlessly cuts through polite evasion and digs up past embarrassments. Where no hard facts can be found, then gossip is simply repeated and the reactions that it generates reported as a means of illuminating character. But this continual digging up of what presumably was hidden ultimately has the effect of destroying the illusion of depth altogether—of cheapening and discrediting it, of turning the idea of the subject from something solid and precious into something fluid and gamelike. For, once we self-consciously accept the notion of our own mystery, once we finally say yes to it, we find that our subsequent reflex is to negate it. We are so schooled, it seems, in finding meaning in the reverse of what is said that when we become truly comfortable with the idea of an unconscious we must suspect that it doesn't exist or that it isn't really us, that it is a creation of ideology, subversive and oppressive. This is precisely the mechanism of postmodern theory in which the quest for meaning is seen around, dismantled, and invalidated as an expression of ideological conditioning. If, under the old (the"modern") dispensation, the individual was made subject to endless interpretation and sanctification, under the new (the "postmodern"), the individual is flattened to a kaleidoscope piece—a fragment in an ever-shifting series of surface patterns, a part of a vast universal ecology, an endless "text."

In talking to my sister and my friend, my tendency was to use their disclaimers as evidence for my interpretation of their unconscious desires and fears. In doing this, I was operating in a modern but not a postmodern mode. Indeed, I feel convinced as I bring this analysis to a close that my method was an anachronism. Perhaps these women did feel a certain way about babies at one time, but now they feel differently. Instead of bringing the past into the present, instead of trying to produce a layered, multivalent meaning, instead of believing in the unconscious of my friends and of myself, I should perhaps accept the present as its own thing, with a perpetual right to turn into something else. In a world with such a rich imagination of calamity as ours, one doesn't want, after all, to get too attached to anything, even to meaning, even to an idea of ourselves—and perhaps not, most of all, to an idea of a child we may be carrying.

Maybe here is where the pro-lifers and the pro-choicers come together. One group wants to literalize the fetus from the moment of conception, making it inaccessible to imaginative interpretation; the other wants to deny it any meaning at all if it is not convenient for the parents to entertain it as meaningful. The notion of being "pregnant"— pregnant with something undefined and mysterious—that, more than anything else, is what is being denied. For to posit, as Freud did, more than the surface, but to leave the interpretation of that "more" open, is to be faced with a responsibility that now may be too much for us to bear.

Confessions of a Literary Daughter

I CAN trace my decision to "go into English" to the experience of a two-semester survey literature course taken during my freshman year in college. I had always loved to read, but that course solidified my interest and set my career path. At the time I probably would have attributed my decision to the power that the books in the course had on me. I now see that the influence lay as much with the professor as with the books.

She was not at all what one would expect an English professor to be. A woman in her sixties, she had a thick Eastern European accent and the figure of a Jewish grandmother. She had lived through the Holocaust, and, at the time I took her course, her husband of thirty years had just left her for a graduate student. She had not been happy in her life, but she had been happy in literature, and she approached Shakespeare and Milton like a priestess before a shrine. I remember her heavily accented voice reading the lines from book 1 of *Paradise Lost* in which Satan, having been defeated in rebellion against God and thrown from Heaven into the "fiery gulf" of Hell, looks around him for the first time:

> "Is this the region, this the soil, the clime,"
> Said then the lost archangel, "this the seat
> That we must change for heaven, this mournful gloom
> For that celestial light? Be it so, since he
> Who now is sovran can dispose and bid
> What shall be right: farthest from him is best . . ."

As our professor read these lines, her voice tremulous with emotion, the class was absolutely silent. "There is," she explained with deliberation afterward, "a certain power to Satan's words in this passage, but ultimately we must dismiss them as the expression of evil: of the blind arrogance of a damned soul." For me, at the time, there was no separating my professor's interpretation from Milton's original intention

143

(that he might have had an unconscious intention didn't occur to me). There was no questioning her assumption that *Paradise Lost* was a great poem, not only a work of genius but also a vehicle for profound and sacred truth. There was no place for discussing whether *Paradise Lost* expressed a repressive culture—a white male Christian scheme to which she had been among the more dramatic victims. I certainly never thought to connect Milton's prestige with my professor's lack of prestige, with the fact that, though she had been on the faculty of this university for some twenty years and had published extensively and well (not to mention the books she had helped her former husband to write), a full professorship had eluded her. My lack of awareness of these things then astounds me now.

But, as much as I can critique my once uncritical acceptance from my present vantage point, I am also the product of that uncritical acceptance. Those lines from *Paradise Lost* as read by that Eastern European voice (and I still hear the accent when I read them to myself) are for me the epitome of great literature and the inspiration behind my choice of a life's work.

This story seems to me to reflect my parentage, to trace certain givens that define me as the daughter of both a father and a mother. Milton and the voice of my English professor are not separable entities for me: their meaning and influence are entwined in my memory and imagination. Although I have become more conscious in recent years of the distinctive emotion-laden voice of the female reader than I was when I first studied *Paradise Lost*, Milton's poem—the text upon which that voice exercised itself—can never be entirely erased from the story. My teacher dropped her husband's name when he left her, but she could not drop her allegiances to Western culture; it had oppressed her and caused her pain, but it had also formed her as a subject and made her a powerful teacher.

I am also the daughter of a real father and mother. My parents are singular, even eccentric, individuals who are nonetheless products of the cultural norms of their generation—a period when gender roles were clearly defined and were supposed to be complementary and hierarchical. The voices of my father and mother resonate behind those I hear when I read; they are the precursors to Milton and my professor.

As their daughter, their product and their mediator, I have been conditioned to hear both voices and to seek, as best I can, to reconcile them.

My father is a scientist by training. After spending his years "at the bench," he went on to serve as director of a succession of corporate R&D programs. He now owns his own chemical company, which he hopes when he retires to sell for a small fortune. The route his life has taken expresses his values: he prizes the scientific method, the hierarchical approach to success, and the bottom line. Had he had a son, he would have expected him to take his own achievements further: to win a Nobel Prize (in chemistry or physics) in his mid-thirties, become CEO of, say, Du Pont in his forties, and wind up his career as a top presidential advisor or cabinet member. He would say that he wanted the same for me. But cues of my childhood argued otherwise.

My mother, my sister, and I were clearly grouped together in my father's mind in a way he was hardly aware of. When he was displeased with one of us, the sense of our conglomerate likeness, our amorphous Otherness to him, bubbled angrily to the surface. At those times, most typically when my mother had failed to buy enough food for a dinner party (my father liked to entertain lavishly and my mother perversely—or perhaps because it was her job to do the preparation, and this was her unconscious means of protest—tended to buy short), he would explode at the three of us, sitting meekly before the insubstantial plate of shrimp that we had helped to arrange. "You people don't know how to do things right," he would lash out, or "I'm fed up with you people." Despite the ostensibly gender-free "you people," I knew that what linked me to my sister and mother in these moments of dissatisfaction in my father's mind was my sex. There was a certain ineptitude basic to my nature that would, hard as I tried to be like him, come to the surface and plague him.

Although my father never ceased to be ambitious for me, to push me toward opportunities and dismiss my fears, his encouragement was always qualified or diverted by the social role he expected me to play. For what he valued above all in my mother, my sister, and me that as clearly marked us as Other as our ineptitude in certain matters of science and common sense were all those talents that dealt in impressions and imprecise calculations. Some of these talents were cultivated through lessons, but the most essential were not teachable in class-rooms. They consisted in the arts of conversation and manners—in a certain social sensitivity and assiduousness, an ability to facilitate the harmonious interaction of those around me. So complete was my initiation in this behavior that I felt inept and uneasy in situations in which no conflict existed for me to mediate, in which I was expected to present myself, simply and straightforwardly, without the friction of other viewpoints to subdue and synthesize. At home I was mostly in my element, for it seemed that my parents fought so that I could help them make up. I was always introduced at their cocktail parties and expected to produce a nice impression, which meant asking good questions of the pompous men and admiring the outfits of their wives. As I grew, my mediating function grew more sophisticated. I became adept at sensing the gaps that existed between people and at filling these in. This meant that I became good, if not at storytelling, then at transitions between stories; if not at speaking, then at listening. I excelled at art, drawing likenesses that elicited wonder (my sister became an adept caricaturist), making landscapes and still lifes that could decorate bare walls, and, not least, making myself as attractive as my native endowments permitted (the emphasis in our household was on what one did with oneself: one complimented a woman by saying she had style or flair, not that she was pretty—that took no work). Most of all, I was expected to be sensitive to language, for it was through this means that I could sense out the desires of others and minister to their needs. My mother likes to tell the story of how her own father, who resembled mine in his admiration for feminine sociability and charm, was sitting in a restaurant with a friend, when their two wives joined them. The women had had a hard day, were tired and less eager to draw out the men than usual. My grandfather grew annoyed. "Mach freulich, wiber" ("Make merry, women"), he instructed them in Yiddish. The phrase remained with my mother and was passed on to me as the answer to the riddle: What do men want from women?

My training in *mach freulich* ultimately led me to play the facilitating role in college and graduate school: completing others' ideas in seminars or taking them to another level of abstraction. My contribution, invariably, was contextual rather than initiating, although in time my sense of context became so acute that it often served as an initiating principle in itself (a point I will return to). It led me to a career as a university critic and teacher in which I mediated texts and students. In the classroom and on department committees, I operated uncannily as I did in my own family. I helped people to see the "other side" or tried for some synthesis of points of view, while always noting the nuance of the personal behind the conventional—the exaggerated liveliness of X's manner, the tension in Y's greeting—and set to work interpreting these signs and smoothing them out. I was drawn to academic life because it allowed me to be feminine in ways that I was taught were acceptable, to put into effect the qualities my father had encouraged me to cultivate, and to deepen and extend their application beyond the realm in which my mother had exercised them.

My mother, a high school French teacher, worked right through my sister's and my growing up despite the frowns of our suburban neighbors. She called herself a feminist before her time, but the perception in the household (as promulgated by my father) was that, as a teacher, she still did women's work. (To do him justice, my father grew immensely proud of my mother as years went by, and she steadily drew a paycheck during his periods between jobs.) But it was true that my mother's fear of risk and her need to have everything under her control were perfectly accommodated within the carefully ordered and circumscribed sphere of her workplace. Although her rebelliousness took the form of scorning cooking and sewing (which she nonetheless did—for who else was there to do these things?—but drew solace by priding herself on doing them badly), her overriding drive was a domestic one. She transformed the site of the local high school where she taught into a kind of alternate household: her tapes, her folders of Xeroxed quizzes and homework sheets, her confrontations and bondings with students, and her elaborate, trivial relations with colleagues were a variation in another key on her life at home with us. In fact, there was no apparent gap in the two worlds my mother inhabited; she stretched them to include each other. Her seven-minute journey between home and work was as automatic to her as her two pieces of buttered toast in the morning, and we seemed to grow up as much in her high school classroom, with its posters of Sartre, Yves Montand, and Degas's ballerinas, as we did in the split-level in which my sister and I shared a bedroom.

It was my mother's job that ultimately became the model for what I could do, and, with the same mix of caution and ingenuity that she had brought to her work, I stepped into the currents of an academic career. Like my mother, I chose to be a teacher, only I bypassed the high school for the university. Like her, I also chose to work with language. But rather than, as she had, studying the subjunctive and irregular verbs of another language, mired as it were in the particular, I chose to delve more deeply into my own and be carried into the realm of "big ideas." The role of literary critic, in what it offers me, seems a metaphor for the way I took my mother's path and extended it, but without really swerving from a conventionally feminine course.

Despite its history as a male occupation, the practice of criticism is feminine insofar as the field has traditionally conceived of itself as subordinate: the critic acting as an interpreter, a mediator, for someone else's words or work. It seems to me significant, however, that, at a time when traditional gender roles are beginning to be redefined, women are increasingly drawn to a critical practice that is on its way to freeing itself from its subordinate status. In a postmodern climate it is not that the critical text is now allowed to be more artful than it once was (although that may superficially appear to be the case); it is that the artistic text to which the critical text had traditionally subordinated itself is being understood to be more like criticism, more of an exercise in textual interpretation in its own right. When all discourse is seen as interpretive, the artistic text and the critical text achieve equality, or, if anything, the heightened awareness associated with criticism gives it priority over an art that remains anchored to traditional attitudes about creativity and originality. Criticism, in other words, is emerging as a form of discourse in which women can continue to perform the mediating role they have been raised to perform, and yet be released from subjugation to an authority that had trivialized that role—made it seem pleasing and helpful but not really important. Criticism, in this sense, is not just an academic pastime; it is an attitude toward experience that is built on ambivalence and ambiguity and a devotion to "good talk"—a discourse open to and capable of incorporating difference and apparent contradiction.

As a critic, I am a derivative of my father, seeking to bring his scientific qualities of mind to the study of cultural materials, to be an entrepreneur of ideas, and to act as a promoter for my own "take" on experience. But my vocation is also an extension of my mother's work. My mother did not compartmentalize or hierarchize. She merely stretched herself to encompass all the activities and responsibilities of her life. The discourse-dominated terrain of postmodernism teaches that interpretation is a powerful tool but a fundamentally domestic one. Its practice consists of the recognition that we are fated to remain always inside the circumscribed space of language, only that space stretches to include everything.

On the Other Hand

I WAS not, I am told, a generous child. My lack of generosity man-
ifested itself most memorably in my behavior with my sister, two
years younger than I and assigned to me by my mother as my beloved
companion. I do not remember ever not loving her or of thinking of her
as less than my best friend—but I was not generous. There is a picture
that I keep on my night table of my sister and me, ages two and four,
respectively. She is in a playpen (a very plain wooden affair; in 1958 little effort was put into dressing up playpens to look less like cages). She
is standing in baggy bermuda shorts, a plain T-shirt and an oversized
cardigan. Her hair is cropped short, and she has a row of very straight
bangs high on her forehead, making her look like a Roman child. She is
facing the camera directly, her expression blank, accepting (perhaps
there is is a trace of a smile on her lips, but I can't be sure). I am standing outside the playpen, smiling widely, aware of the camera but not
concerned about it, squinting in the sunshine. My tanktop is striped
and pulled tight across my chest, and my hair is in careless wisps
around my face. I am holding—and here's where the pathos of the picture really lies—a string of beads and wearing two or three strands
around my neck. The expressiveness and lavishness that attaches to my
image as it contrasts the spartan, enigmatic appearance of my sister is,
to the practiced eye of my family, wholly characteristic of our person-
alities and very moving. I learned to read that picture when I was quite
young. It, along with certain stories about how I wouldn't share my
crayons, was instrumental in defining me as selfish—in a benign way,
mind you (my family was definite but never harsh in its judgments,
which may have been why they were so effective). I feel that the way in
which I was taught to read this photograph stands behind my present
tendency to qualify and contradict myself. For my style is a verbal sharing, perhaps a way I found to avoid having really to share, perhaps an
amends I discovered for that early reputation of selfishness.

To have a sister, as I explain elsewhere in these essays, is to always
have an echo. I stand outside the playpen next to my sister within. That

picture seems to encode a series of shifting opposites involving freedom and constraint, power and powerlessness, anger and guilt. It
defines me as outside: free, gluttonous, sun soaked. But it also defines
me as an outsider to the enigmatic visage and to the whole framed icon
that is my sister inside the playpen. Sometimes, lately, when I return to
study that photograph, I find that my smile seems less bacchanalian,
seems, on the contrary, confused, distracted, even anxious. My once
jaunty-appearing stance beside the playpen now appears less balanced
and centered: I seem to be leaning for support on that structure, while
my sister stands solidly planted within. Even the beads, the emblem of
my selfishness, can tell another story; for, if you look closely, you see
that they are very small, probably glass, not at all the kind of thing you
want a two-year-old to play with. It is an observation that suggests to
me that perhaps the strand I am holding is the sign of my protective-
ness toward my sister, that in my anxiety I have just retrieved it from
her (this is an interpretation that could only have occurred to me after I
became a mother).

This revisionist interpretation appeals to me and fits well with certain tendencies toward anxiety and overprotectiveness that I have
begun to discern in myself in recent years, and yet it also makes me
uncomfortable. I don't like its clean revisionary lines. It seems ungen-
erous in granting me too dramatic a role in the scene and in smugly top-
pling a family mythology—hence, I can see it supporting my family's
earlier assessment of me. Yet I can store this new reading without
embracing it entirely; indeed, if each new interpretation liberates me
somewhat from the one before, there still remains a trace of that earlier
reading that I must continue to reckon with. Having once been labeled
selfish, I will always think about whether or not I am. Having once
identified myself as a mother, I will always weigh whether protective
feelings enter into my actions toward another person. Each interpretation throws up a possibility for meaning that must be filed away and,
when a new experience happens, taken out and examined for a possible fit.

What I finally get from contemplating the old photograph is the
sense that my place in the family and my relationship to my sister are
not simple or single or static, that they are capable of assimilating a
variety of ostensibly contradictory meanings and that those meanings
will continue to be generated as long as I live. What strikes me about

this understanding of the picture is the way it takes what I do as a literary critic and turns it back on myself. It allows me to qualify the meaning of my own past as I have qualified the reading of literary texts through context and experience.

But I also see my method as extending beyond myself and reflecting a cultural moment. If the nineteenth century was an age of ideology and the twentieth century an age of interpretation, the twenty-first century may be an age of qualification. Qualification, unlike interpretation, never discards what came before; it simply assimilates it into a larger design. It is a form of linguistic imperialism that, unlike other forms of imperialism, has as its goal not power but inclusiveness. It is this democratizing aspect of qualification that allies it with tendencies associated with postmodernism. In the present cultural climate all positions take on a certain shifting, relative validity as we are continually made to recognize the patchwork quality not only of our antagonists' arguments but also of our own. In such a climate debate as such ceases, and what we have instead is dialogue—and, above all, internal dialogue: a continual examination of the motives and meanings behind what we say. Qualification is this continual self-assessment and self-adjustment transferred to the level of style.

Women, of course, have always been associated with qualified speech. This has been seen to reflect their doubt and insecurity as a marginalized group. Yet this kind of labeling only makes sense within a traditional competitive system in which one person's meaning is understood to exist at the expense of another's. Such a system obviously prevails in many pockets of our culture, but it is also beginning to be questioned as the nuclear family undergoes revision and organizational configurations become more varied and open. The authoritative voice of the father is being modulated; the voice of the mother is being heard; and the daughter is being empowered to blend those voices in her own way. In this context qualification is not an expression of powerlessness but of creative self-definition, a valuing but also an assimilation of difference.

In these essays I have tried to express my debt to a mother and a father as these influences have filtered to me from my family and from the books and cultural artifacts that have meant most to me. I have tried to qualify each influence by noting its connectedness to other things and to shape a self I can live with and continue to revise. This process of revision has already begun. As I look back on these essays, I find them to be both familiar and strange. I know them to be mine, and yet I feel myself receding from them, having ceased to be the person I was when I wrote them. The thoughts and emotions that once seemed so pressing have lost their urgency and mutated into other thoughts and emotions. The sense of urgency, the site of selfhood, lies elsewhere. I have become a reader engaged in sometimes sympathetic, sometimes angry, dialogue with my own words, now prepared to write from a new place.

Notes

The following are informal notes, keyed to each essay, providing bibliographical information on the secondary sources referred to and directing interested readers to more theoretical or fact-based studies on related topics. I acknowledge that personal taste and whimsy direct many of the references here; it would be impossible to be comprehensive within such a broad and much-traveled terrain.

Novels, poems, and culturally enshrined critical texts are not fully referenced, since they are readily available in bookstores and libraries, often in a variety of editions.

Introduction

Some noteworthy titles in the growing genre of autobiographical literary criticism include Rachel M. Brownstein's *Becoming a Heroine: Reading about Women in Novels* (New York: Viking, 1982); Nancy K. Miller's *Getting Personal: Feminist Occasions and Other Autobiographical Acts* (New York: Routledge, 1991); Alice Kaplan's *French Lessons: A Memoir* (Univ. of Chicago Press, 1993); Marianna De Marco Torgovnick's *Crossing Ocean Parkway: Readings by an Italian American Daughter* (Univ. of Chicago Press, 1994); and the anthology *The Intimate Critique: Autobiographical Literary Criticism*, ed. Diane P. Freedman, Olivia Frey, and Frances Murphy Zauhar (Durham: Duke Univ. Press, 1993), which includes a revised version of Jane Tompkins's much-cited manifesto of autobiographical literary criticism, "Me and My Shadow" (1988). Other, less academic contributions to the genre include Adrienne Rich's *On Lies, Secrets, and Silence: 1966–78* (New York: Norton, 1979); Gloria Anzaldúa's *Borderlands / La Frontera: The New Mestiza* (San Francisco: Spinsters/aunt lute, 1987); Alice Walker's *In Search of Our Mother's Gardens: Womanist Prose* (New York: Harvest, 1984); Camille Paglia's *Sex, Art, and American Culture* (New York: Vintage, 1992); and Janet Malcolm's delicious amalgam of biography and autobiography, *The Silent Woman: Sylvia Plath and Ted Hughes* (New York: Knopf, 1994).

Poetry and Sexual Harassment

Each side of the sexual harassment debate that this essay considers has vocal and eloquent advocates. On one side are feminist scholars and activists such as Catherine MacKinnon and Susan Faludi, who see harassment as an unrelenting and pervasive facet of women's experience under patriarchy; on the other side are the likes of Katie Roiphe and Camille Paglia, self-professed "new feminists" who believe such views infantilize women and ignore the complexity of human relationships. That the two sides have been showcased on talk shows and in magazines suggests to me less that the issue is polarized (though this may be true in some pockets of the college campus) than that the public is ambivalent and capable of seeing both sides.

How a woman reads in a patriarchal culture has been a subject of feminist discussion for a long time. The idea of "reading against the grain" of the male or male-conditioned text was initially articulated by feminist literary critics such as Elaine Showalter and Annette Kolodny. The French theorist Julia Kristeva's notion of the "semiotic" brought a psychoanalytic dimension to the discussion. Contributions have also come from the field of film theory, beginning perhaps with Laura Mulvey's 1975 essay, "Visual Pleasure and Narrative Cinema" (rpt. in Mulvey's *Visual and Other Pleasures* [Bloomington: Indiana Univ. Press, 1989]), which sees the female spectator as split between her identification with the position of the generic male observer and her identification with the female object on the screen.

"To Hell with Dying"

I quote from Alice Walker's essay "The Black Writer and the Southern Experience" in her collection *In Search of Our Mothers' Gardens: Womanist Prose*. Robert Pattison's *The Child Figure in English Literature* (Athens: Univ. of Georgia Press, 1978) offers a scholarly, thematic treatment of the child's perspective as a literary technique.

Sisters

Readers should note that John Halperin's biography *The Life of Jane Austen* (Baltimore: Johns Hopkins Univ. Press, 1984) has since been followed by a more Austen-friendly one, Park Honan's *Jane Austen: Her Life* (New York: St. Martin's, 1987), which makes a point of crediting Cassandra's role in the novelist's development. Deborah Kaplan's *Jane Austen among Women* (Baltimore: Johns Hopkins Univ. Press, 1992) also discusses how Austen was supported by a "women's culture" that managed to ignore or flout many of the values of the patriarchal culture. Also of interest is Helena Mitchie's *Sororaphobia: Differences among Women in Literature and Culture* (New York: Oxford Univ. Press, 1992), which deconstructs the notion of sisterhood in Western culture.

Quotes from Austen's letters come from *Jane Austen's Letters to Her Sister Cassandra and Others*, ed. R. W. Chapman (London: Oxford Univ. Press, 1979).

Turning the Screw on Dr. Spock

Barbara Ehrenreich and Deirdre English's *For Her Own Good: 150 Years of the Experts' Advice to Women* (Garden City, N.Y.: Anchor, 1978) remains for me the classic on female conditioning in the maternal role. I quote from chapter 6, "The Century of the Child." The pioneering feminist theoretical work on the psychological basis and effects of mothering is Nancy Chodorow's *Reproduction of Mothering: Psychoanalysis and the Sociology of Gender* (Berkeley: Univ. of Calif. Press, 1978).

Although my essay voices skepticism about Dr. Spock and other experts, some of the recent guides to child rearing are less prescriptive than discursive and reassuring. My current favorite is Mary Sheedy Krucinka's *Raising the Spirited Child: A Guide for Parents Whose Child is More Intense, Sensitive, Perceptive, Persistent, Energetic* (New York: HarperCollins, 1991). What parent could resist a title like that?

On Henry James and his family the output is voluminous. I would cite Leon Edel's five-volume biography, *Henry James* (Philadelphia: J. B. Lippincott, 1953–72) as still the best interweaving of biography, literary criticism, and psychological analysis. Jean Strouse's *Alice James: A Biography* (Boston: Houghton Mifflin, 1980) and Howard M. Feinstein's *Becoming William James* (Ithaca, N.Y.: Cornell Univ. Press, 1984) are excellent at providing deeper insights into the dynamics of the James family. I quote from Edmund Wilson's essay "The Ambiguity of Henry James" in *The Triple Thinkers* (New York: Penguin, 1962).

An additional note: I am aware of my periodic use of *we* and *one* in this essay and in others in this volume and know that both terms have their pitfalls: *we* may presumptuously suggest too great a homogeneity in my audience; *one* may give an impression of seamless authority— what I am generally at pains to avoid. Yet I have found no satisfying alternative. I wonder whether the use of *we* and *one* isn't built into the critic's vocabulary and that the best "we" can do is vary the use of these terms as much as possible. See Marianna De Marco Torgovnick's discussion of the problem of "we" in her chapter, "The Politics of 'We,'" in *Crossing Ocean Parkway.*

Anorexic Thinking

On the subject of anorexia Hilde Bruch's *The Golden Cage: The Enigma of Anorexia Nervosa* (Cambridge: Harvard Univ. Press, 1978) is a succinct clinical and anecdotal introduction, and Joan Jacobs Brumberg's *Fasting Girls: The Emergence of Anorexia Nervosa as a Modern Disease* (Cambridge: Harvard Univ. Press, 1988) is a comprehensive historical overview. Sandra M. Gilbert and Susan Gubar, in *The Madwoman in the Attic: The Woman Writer and the Nineteenth-Century Literary Imagination* (New Haven: Yale Univ. Press, 1979), seem to have been the first to discuss the illness in a literary context.

I quote from Sylvia Plath's "Lady Lazarus," Louise Glück's "Dedication to Hunger," and Dickinson's poem #642.

The Good Class

Despite the many books written over the past fifteen years dealing with higher education, few look closely at classroom dynamics from a personal rather than a prescriptive standpoint. One exception is the excellent, still timely monograph, *Literature and the English Department*, by Barrett John Mandel (Champaign, Ill.: National Council of Teachers of English, 1970). I also recommend Peter Elbow's *Embracing Contraries: Exploration in Learning and Teaching* (New York: Oxford Univ. Press, 1986) and Rosetta Marantz Cohen's ethnographic study of the good teacher, *A Lifetime of Teaching* (New York: Teachers College Press, 1991). For specific pedagogical insights into teaching Blake's *Songs*, see Robert F. Gleckner and Mark L. Greenberg's *Approaches to Teaching Blake's*

"Songs of Innocence and of Experience" (New York: Modern Language Association, 1989).

Speech and Silence

Women's speech as it differs from men's has been a subject of research by feminist scholars for over a decade. The most notable contributions in this area are Carol Gilligan's *In a Different Voice: Psychological Theory and Women's Development* (Cambridge: Harvard Univ. Press, 1982); Mary Field Belenky, Blyth McVicker Clinchy, Nancy Rule Goldberger, and Jill Mattuck Tarule's *Women's Ways of Knowing: The Development of Self, Voice, and Mind* (New York: Basic Books, 1986); and Deborah Tannen's series of more popular books on the subject, the most recent being *Talking from 9 to 5: How Women's and Men's Conversational Styles Affect Who Gets Heard, Who Gets Credit, and What Gets Done* (New York: William Morrow, 1994). On the Jewish voice in America, see Ruth R. Wisse, *The Schlemiel as Modern Hero* (Univ. of Chicago Press, 1971) and on the black voice, see *Reading Black, Reading Feminist: A Critical Anthology*, ed. Henry Louis Gates (New York: Meridian, 1990). I quote from Deborah E. McDowell's essay in Gates's collection,"'The Changing Same': Generational Connections and Black Women Novelists."

For a feminist deconstruction of the western, see Jane Tompkins's *West of Everything: The Inner Life of Westerns* (New York: Oxford Univ. Press, 1992).

Rx for Premature Labor: Reading Trollope

Feeding my discomfort in my original assessment of Trollope is the fact that he has been steadily gaining defenders in recent years. No less than four biographies by notable scholars have appeared since James Pope Hennessy's in 1971, of which the latest, Victoria Glendinning's *Anthony Trollope* (New York: Knopf, 1993), is probably the most vigorously supportive.

My citations from Erich Auerbach's *Mimesis: The Representation of Reality in Western Literature*, trans. Willard R. Trask (Princeton Univ. Press, 1968), are from the chapter "Odysseus' Scar."

The Marriage Plot

The marriage plot in novels has been fertile ground for analysis by feminist critics and narrative theorists. A sampling of work in this area, written over the past fifteen years, includes Carolyn G. Heilbrun's "Marriage Perceived: English Literature, 1873–1941" (cited in my essay), in *What Manner of Woman: Essays on English and American Life and Literature*, ed. Marlene Springer (New York Univ. Press, 1977); Nancy K. Miller's *The Heroine's Text* (New York: Columbia Univ. Press, 1980); Rachel M. Brownstein's *Becoming a Heroine* (also cited); D. A. Miller's *Narrative and Its Discontents* (Princeton Univ. Press, 1981); and Joseph Allen Boone's *Tradition Counter Tradition: Love and the Form of Fiction* (Univ. of Chicago Press, 1987).

Referred to in passing are Phyllis Rose's *Parallel Lives: Five Victorian Marriages* (New York: Vintage, 1984); Diana Trilling's *The Beginning of the Journey: The Marriage of Lionel and Diana Trilling* (New York: Viking, 1993); and Nigel Nicolson's *Portrait of a Marriage* (New York: Atheneum, 1973). I quote from Nicolson's introduction.

Born to Shop

I quote from Lionel Trilling's "Manners, Morals, and the Novel," in *The Liberal Imagination* (Garden City, N.Y.: Doubleday, 1953); and Gregory Bateson's "The Group Dynamics of Schizophrenia," in *Steps to an Ecology of Mind* (New York: Ballantine, 1972).

On Reading Proust

For me, admittedly no expert on Proust, two accessible and still provocative discussions of the novelist remain René Girard's *Deceit, Desire, and the Novel: Self and Other in Literary Structure*, trans. Yvonne Freccero (Baltimore: Johns Hopkins Univ. Press, 1965); and Germaine Brée's *Marcel Proust and Deliverance from Time* (New Brunswick, N.J.: Rutgers Univ. Press, 1969). My taste for Wordsworth was formed in college in the 1970s and owes a great deal to Geoffrey Hartman's *Wordsworth's Poetry, 1787–1814* (New Haven: Yale Univ. Press, 1964).

"Makin' Whoopee": The Art of Female Self-Performance

I quote from the chapter "Performing Heroinism: The Myth of Corinne," in Ellen Moers's *Literary Women* (Garden City, N.Y.: Anchor, 1977).

Naomi Wolf presents a critique of the auto-aesthetic in *The Beauty Myth: How Images of Beauty Are Used Against Women* (New York: Anchor, 1991), and Camille Paglia offers her inimitable take on the subject of self-performance in her essays on Madonna in *Sex, Art, and American Culture*. Also see Wendy Lesser's excellent collection of essays, *His Other Half: Men Looking at Women through Art* (Cambridge: Harvard Univ. Press, 1991), for a discussion of related issues.

Love and Pity

See Peter Middleton, *The Inward Gaze: Masculinity and Subjectivity in Modern Culture* (New York: Routledge, 1992), for an academic discussion of some related points about the limitations built into conventional masculinity.

The citation about Andrew Jackson is from Paul Johnson's *The Birth of the Modern: World Society, 1815–1830* (New York: HarperCollins, 1991), from the chapter "The Congress Dances."

The Birth and Death of the Unconscious

This essay deals with an evolution of consciousness that has been treated extensively by cultural theorists, beginning perhaps with Michel Foucault's *History of Sexuality*, vol. 1: *An Introduction*, trans. Robert Hurley (New York: Vintage, 1981), and reaching its apotheosis in Jean-François Lyotard's *The Postmodern Condition: A Report on Knowledge* (Minneapolis: Univ. of Minnesota Press, 1984). A powerful critique of postmodern thinking can be found in Arthur Kroker and David Cook's *The Postmodern Scene: Excremental Culture and Hyper-Aesthetics* (New York: St. Martin's Press, 1986).

I quote from Dorothea Krook's chapter on *The Golden Bowl* (I) in *The Ordeal of Consciousness in Henry James* (Cambridge Univ. Press, 1962).

Confessions of a Literary Daughter

My interest in the daughter's case began as a scholarly examination of the nineteenth-century novel and family in *The Daughter's Dilemma: Family Process and the Nineteenth-Century Domestic Novel* (Ann Arbor: Univ. of Michigan Press, 1991). The book concentrates primarily on the father-daughter dynamic as it has evolved in Western culture. On the same subject, I also recommend Lynda E. Boose and Betty S. Flowers's edited collection, *Daughters and Fathers* (Baltimore: Johns Hopkins Univ. Press, 1989). On the mother-daughter relationship in literature, see Marianne Hirsch's *The Mother-Daughter Plot: Narrative, Psychoanalysis, Feminism* (Bloomington: Indiana Univ. Press, 1989).

On the Other Hand

Again, see Gilligan, *In a Different Voice;* Belenky et al., *Women's Ways of Knowing;* and Tannen, *Talking from 9 to 5,* for further discussion of qualification as a female linguistic style. For a provocative discussion of the affect of feminism on the critic, see Stephen Heath's essay, "Male Feminism," in *Men in Feminism,* ed. Alice Jardine and Paul Smith (New York: Methuen, 1987).